MARTELLO TOWERS

MICHAEL FOLEY

AMBERLEY

*To the person who was instrumental in convincing me that
I should carry on writing when I had doubts: Reg Allington,
my English teacher from school, who could instil confidence
in all his pupils no matter what their backgrounds were.*

First published 2013

Amberley Publishing
The Hill, Stroud
Gloucestershire, GL5 4EP

www.amberleybooks.com

British Library Cataloguing in Publication Data.
A catalogue record for this book is available from the British Library.

ISBN 978 1 4456 1522 6 (print)
ISBN 978 1 4456 1545 5 (ebook)

Typeset in 10pt on 12pt Sabon.
Typesetting and Origination by Amberley Publishing.
Printed in the UK.

CONTENTS

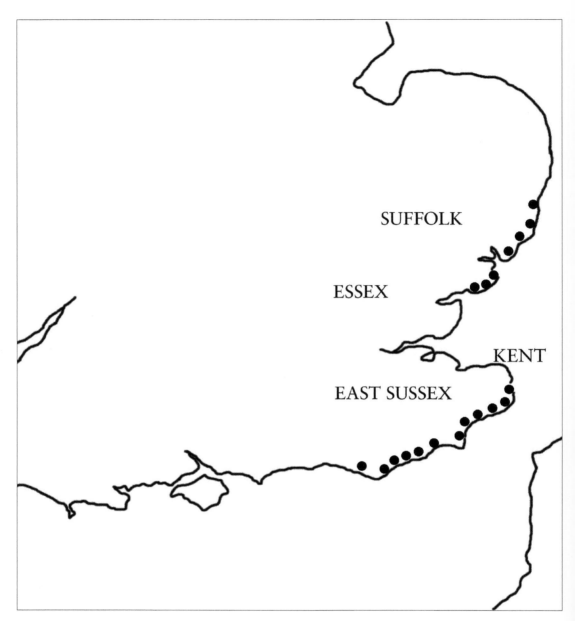

Approximate positions of surviving South and East Coast towers.

ACKNOWLEDGEMENTS

I would like to thank the following people for their kind help in compiling this book in a number of different ways. First, Gillian Newman and Paul McNicol at Hastings Reference Library for their help in locating newspaper articles concerning Martello towers in the Hastings area. I would also like to thank Kerry Meal of Lowestoft Record Office for her hard work in helping to locating documents and articles on the Martello towers in Suffolk. To Mary McGillicuddy, Steve Popple, Ron Strutt and the staff of the Felixstowe School for Girls for the use of their photographs, and to John Weedy of www.iln.org.uk for finding a copy of a print that I had lost. To Simon Fletcher for his work on the text. Thank you to Alan Filtness, Andrew Monks and Reg Allington for helping me to locate and get to the existing towers, so that I could take the photographs that appear in this book. This ensured that I saw every remaining tower in Suffolk, Essex, Kent and Sussex. Reading about something is never a substitute for seeing it for yourself.

The Author

Michael Foley's website can be found at http://www.michael-foley-history-writer.co.uk/ His previous titles from Amberley Publishing include:

Essex at War Through Time
Havering Through Time
Barking & Dagenham Through Time
East London Through Time
Essex Through Time
Essex at War From Old Photographs

INTRODUCTION

The Napoleonic Martello Towers of the South and South East Coast

There are a large number of old buildings that stretch along the South and East Coast of our country. They are all very similar in appearance. They have been around for such a long time that many people walk past them over and over again without noticing them. Those who do pay attention often mistake them for water towers or even ventilation shafts of some kind, which is understandable because of their shape. Another reason that many people do not know what they are is that there has been very little written about them, and what has been written is usually only read by those who are interested in the period in which they were built.

These buildings are Martello towers, defences built to combat the threat of invasion from Napoleon and his mighty army during the French wars of the late eighteenth and early nineteenth centuries. There were originally more than 100 of them in the four counties of Suffolk, Essex, Kent and Sussex, which were seen as the most likely spots for a French landing. Unfortunately the historical importance of these buildings was not recognised until relatively recently, and less than half of them survive.

The level of interest displayed by the public in these towers has varied over time. When Daisy Elfreda Lynes wrote her children's novel *The Martello Tower* in the late 1930s (under the pseudonym D. Glyn-Forest), no doubt her readers were children who still learnt about our country's history in schools. They would have known what she was talking about when she mentioned Martello towers. The fascination that the characters showed for the towers would no doubt have been shared by many children of the period. (It is difficult, by the way, to work out which tower the author was writing about, if indeed the book is based on a particular tower. The clues regarding location indicate the tower at Aldeburgh, but it is described as one of the more normal towers – which Aldeburgh wasn't. Perhaps this is intentional on the author's part.)

The Martello towers were controversial from the time they were planned, and their construction was criticised shortly after their erection as well as much later in their history. This was because they were never actually used to defend the coast from the French. The threat of invasion was to be no more than that: a threat. Whether their presence had a part to play in the failure of the French to invade cannot be judged. But the critics fail to mention that the towers played a useful role in defending the coast against smuggling, both in the time of the Coastal Blockade after the Napoleonic Wars and by the Coastguard later on.

Criticism of defensive structures in this country has not been limited to the Martello towers. A number of forts built in the 1860s became known as Palmerston's Follies because they also never faced an enemy. If this is the criterion used to judge the effectiveness of defences then one should also criticise those erected during the First and Second World Wars. Would the critics have felt better if we had been invaded, purely because these defences would have played a more active role?

When the Dutch attacked England in the seventeenth century they sailed up the Thames and into the Medway, where they destroyed a half-built fort at Sheerness and took many of the British Navy's best ships as prizes. London was thrown into widespread panic in case they sailed upriver to the capital. At one point the only defence standing between the Dutch fleet and London was an out-of-date and poorly armed fort at Tilbury. This shows what can happen if defences are either absent or not

Pubd. by T. S. Gowland, Library, Eastbourne.

An old print of the Wish Tower in Eastbourne (to the right). Just visible to the left of the print are the line of towers that once existed along the Sussex coast.

well maintained. If the Martello towers had not been built and the French had come, criticism of the government would have been much worse.

Many Martello towers were built in very secluded spots, the places where enemy troops were likely to land. Many were later occupied by the Coastal Blockade men, whose work came under the command of the Navy. These remote locations were inevitably those used by smugglers. The danger that these blockade men experienced was greater than that of any garrison occupying the towers during the Napoleonic Wars.

The history of the individual towers varies greatly. Some disappeared soon after they were built without leaving much of a history behind them. There were various reasons for this. The sea encroached on some, others were demolished to make way for new buildings, and some were victims of Royal Artillery testing of guns and explosives. Of those that survive some have been altered and are now homes – dramatically standing out among more normal houses – while others have been turned into small museums, but a large number are now standing derelict and unused. It is these that are most likely to be ignored.

At last the importance of the Martello towers is now being recognised, and it is highly unlikely that any more will be lost to demolition – although some are still in danger from nature. Coastal erosion is an ever-growing threat, with global warming leading to rising sea levels – and the protection of ancient buildings becomes less justifiable when the cost of new coastal defences runs into millions of pounds. We should therefore make the most of these buildings while they still exist.

1

THE HISTORICAL BACKGROUND

It is commonly believed that British Martello towers were based on a tower at a place called Mortella Point, which overlooks a bay on the island of Corsica. Some writers have even named this bay, scene of a battle between the French defenders of the tower and British warships in the late eighteenth century, Mortella Bay. This tale begins most short histories of the Martello towers, but may not be the complete story; other writers give more detail.

An article by Commander Hilary Mead RN written in 1948 includes two quotes but unfortunately just the names of their authors, not the sources. The first is from 1826 and someone named James: 'This extraordinary tower is named Mortella after its inventor.' The second is from Brenton: 'Some of the Martello Towers stood in this bay but whether they imparted their name to it or derived their name from the anchorage I have not been able to determine.' Therefore it seems unclear if the area was named after the tower or the tower was named after the area. Another view is given by Glendinning, who places this first tower in Corsica's Gulf of Fiorenzo, now known as the Gulf of St Florent. He claims that there was also a tower at Cape Mortella, but this was not the one attacked by the British but on the island of Capraja (now called Caraia), guarding a prison colony. This was also known to the British as Nelson occupied the island in 1796. Perhaps the tower that was attacked by the British was called a Mortella tower after the one on Caraia, and its location became known as Mortella Point after the tower, rather than the tower taking its name from its site.

The situation is made even more confused because there were a number of similar towers around the Mediterranean, including a large number on the coast of Italy. The tower on Caraia was close to those on the coast of Genoa, for example – originally watchtowers to keep a lookout for pirates, built hundreds of years before. These may have had bells to warn of danger, and a bell has a clapper or hammer, in Italian a *martello*. I leave you to make up your own mind about this.

Yet another idea, put forward by Victor J. Enoch, is that the towers are named after the shrub myrtle, which grows near the tower that was attacked by the British. He claims that in Corsica myrtle is called mortella.

Whatever the reason for its name, there seems little doubt that the tower attacked by the British really did become known as a Mortella tower. It is claimed that this name was misspelt by a member of the British Navy, thereby becoming Martello.

The origins of the tower at Mortella Point had much to do with the Mediterranean watchtowers that stretched back into the ancient past, built as lookout posts to guard

The Torre dello Ziro, an ancient watchtower on the Amalfi Coast of Italy. It was used to watch for Saracen pirates but in the sixteenth century it was used as a prison for Giovanna D'Aragona, the Duchess of Amalfi, and her children, who were then murdered there.

against pirates, and the Saracens. The common trait of these towers and the later Martellos is the entrance set high in the walls with a temporary or easily destroyed wooden set of steps. This made it more difficult for an attacking force to gain entry, even if the tower was only lightly armed.

Along the Italian coast these towers, known originally as Saracen or Corsair towers, were built from the eleventh century, and between Gaeta and Amalfi there were more than 350 of them. Many survive today. There are also many in Spain. These were first built by the Moors, also to watch for pirates, and were later used by the Christian population after the Moors had been expelled, to warn the population of any attempt to re-conquer them by their former masters.

The watchtowers often worked in conjunction with each other. They had a flat roof on which a signal fire could be lit to raise the alarm, and to send signals from one tower to the next, rather than a cannon for defence. The Martello towers later built in England co-operated in the same way, with each being built in sight of others for support; an attacking ship would come under the fire of several towers at once.

Although the use of towers and castles as coastal defences declined in Europe during the Middle Ages, especially with the arrival of artillery, the situation changed again by the time of the French wars of the late eighteenth and early nineteenth centuries,

The site of the Torre dello Ziro shows that it is not a defensive building, as it is too far from the sea, but is a lookout position.

when it became obvious that towers still had a part to play. The British force in Corsica learnt this through the events that took place there.

Any invasion force from France was likely to come in the shape of small boats rather than large ships. The towers could deal with these, although it was shown at Mortella Point that they could also defeat (or at least hinder) large ships as well.

The tower in Corsica came to the notice of the British during the French occupation of the island in 1793. The Corsican patriot General Paoli asked for British help against the French forces, and in response British ships arrived at the Gulf of San Fiorenzo. Here they found the tower manned by the French. Although most accounts concentrate on this one tower, which the British besieged, other accounts (such as that of Hogg) state that there were actually three old watchtowers in the bay.

At this time Corsica was in a state of upheaval. A report in *The Times* in July 1793 stated that the French had been disarmed and that General Paoli was in command of the island, but by April the following year the same newspaper stated that the French under the command of Colonel d'Aubant were besieging Baftin. It was during this campaign that Nelson lost his eye. The final outcome was not in favour of General Paoli, who ended his days in England as a guest of George III after being driven out of Corsica by his enemies. He died aged eighty-two in April 1807.

The Corsican tower was first taken in 1793 after it had been bombarded by HMS *Lowestoft*. That it fell to just one ship does not seem that impressive, and surely indicates that it would not have had any influence on British plans for coastal defence. The tower was handed over to Corsican patriots, who were trying to keep the island independent of the French, but unfortunately the tower was taken again, without too much trouble it seems, and was manned once more by the French.

The following year the British returned, this time with the thirty-two-gun HMS *Juno* and the larger HMS *Fortitude* with seventy-two guns. This time the resistance they found was much stronger. The ships opened fire on the tower but the French retaliated with heated shot, causing an explosion on one of the ships. Both ships eventually retired from the battle, with six dead and almost sixty wounded. A force of 1,400 men was then landed, along with four artillery pieces, under the command of Major-General Dundas and Lieutenant-General Moore. They fired on the tower for two days before what seems to have been a lucky shot started a fire, at which point the defending force surrendered. A grand total of thirty-three men had fought off two ships and 1,400 men.

Why the defence of the tower in 1794 was so much stronger than on previous occasions is unclear. Perhaps the men just had more courage than their predecessors. There is no doubt, however, that this event played a part in the later construction of many of the similar towers in Britain. A number of the senior officers who made decisions regarding the building of these English towers were present at the Mortella Point attack, and it may well be that their experience influenced the building of the English towers. Admiral Sir John Jervis, later Lord St Vincent, wrote in 1796 that Martello towers were needed in Britain – he 'hoped to see such works erected on every part of the [English] coast likely for an enemy to make a descent on'. At the same time a Captain Pakenham was preparing a model of the tower in Corsica for the Master-General of Ordnance, Marquis Cornwallis.

A very old postcard of Langney Point, Sussex, showing a ruined tower and a line of towers that no longer all exist.

Such an apparently important event, especially in the context of future British home defences, does not seem to have merited a mention in *The Times*, although a number of articles about Corsica appeared in the newspaper at this time. It seems that either the attack on the tower was too insignificant to warrant a mention, or that a poorly manned tower holding off a strong British force was not what the military wanted the public to read about.

Another event in Corsica involved a Martello tower. On 1 May 1811 three British ships, the frigates *Pomone* and *Unite* and the sloop *Scout*, made an attack on three large French store ships, which were in port and were protected by a four-gun battery, a Martello tower with a large gun and 200 troops with field guns. In a conflict lasting an hour and a half the British force destroyed the three French ships, the battery and the Martello tower, with the loss of only two dead and twenty-five wounded. If the great show put up by the tower in 1794 had such a positive influence on British defences, why did the poor show this time not have a negative effect? It may have been too late for the mainland towers, which were already built, but other towers were constructed later.

It would seem that the usefulness of such defensive structures was common knowledge before events in Corsica, as Martello towers were not just constructed on the British mainland. It is clear that the incident at Mortella Point did not lead to the instant erection of similar towers around the coasts of Britain: the idea was already well ingrained by the end of the eighteenth century.

Although there is debate whether they can truly be described as Martello towers, many were built on the Channel Islands – some of them before the battle at Mortella Point in 1794. Despite being slightly different in design, they have come to be grouped

The Channel Islands had towers before the mainland that became known as Martellos although many differed in design. One is commemorated on this Guernsey stamp.

together with the later towers. It also appears that the name Martello was not applied to these Channel Islands towers until some years after the first towers on the mainland were built, and that they were previously known as sea towers. However, press reports use the word Martello in conjunction with towers built in Ireland at this time.

The Channel Islands had always been close to the old enemy France and had a number of defences. These were added to in 1778 when twenty-three round towers were built on Jersey thanks to the governor of the island, General Conway. There had originally been plans for thirty. They did not stop an attempted French invasion in 1779, which was repulsed. The defences were updated two years later, one fort being paid for by merchants and businessmen on the island. The towers on Jersey differed from the later Martello towers in that they were designed for protection by soldiers with muskets, mainly because of a shortage of cannon on the islands.

This was followed by fifteen towers on Guernsey. These were more like the Mediterranean watchtowers than the later Martello towers on the mainland, but were grouped under the same name later. The amazing thing is that the towers on Guernsey seem to have been built in a year, and the price of the construction of the towers on Jersey was given as £156 each. This was quicker and cheaper by far than the later mainland towers. Costs were kept down on the islands because the land on which most of the towers were built did not have to be paid for – as it was either common land or the seashore, which was seen to belong to everyone.

Although most of the Channel Island towers were built in the late eighteenth century, this one, Kempt Tower in St Ouen's Bay, Jersey, wasn't built until 1834.

A 1787 report on fortification of the islands described towers as the best form of defence, and was signed by (among others) Robert Morse and Colonel Abraham D. Aubent, later present at the incident at Mortella Point. Perhaps, then, it was not the events in Corsica that were the spur to building the towers on the mainland. Perhaps some of those present there had already been convinced of the usefulness of towers, and the Mortella Point incident just reinforced that belief rather than being a defining influence.

A further report on defences in 1804 led to more towers being built on Guernsey. The cost, although it had risen steeply, was still much cheaper than it was to be on the mainland – just £500 each – and this may be one of the reasons why the construction of the mainland towers was so severely criticised. More towers were also built in Jersey, as they were on the other islands until the 1830s.

In 1795 two towers were built in South Africa at the Cape of Good Hope, shortly after the area was taken by the British and when they feared an attack by the French or the Dutch. The man in command of the British forces was Vice-Admiral George Elphinstone, who had also been present at the Corsican Mortella incident. The following year Prince Edward, later the Duke of York, built a round tower in Nova Scotia. By 1798 two more towers had been built in Canada. In 1797 a tower was built on Ladder Hill in remote St Helena, an important stopping post for British ships on the way to South Africa. It was manned by troops from the East India Company, which at this time owned the island.

Sir Charles Stuart captured Minorca in 1798, and a number of round towers were built on the island by the occupying British forces, adding to the old watchtowers that already existed. The first seven were built under Stuart, another eight under his successors. Four of the first seven were built to protect Mahon, while the other three were located where the British had landed when they took the island. The others were scattered around the island, which for a time was the most important British naval base in the Mediterranean. The Royal Engineer in command of building the towers in Minorca was Captain Robert D'Arcy, also in Corsica at the time of the Mortella Point conflict. Up to this point the towers had been of several different designs, but the Minorcan towers were similar to those later built on the English coast. In 1800 Abercrombie's expedition to Egypt was assembled on Minorca, which would have given all those involved a chance to see the towers at first hand. No doubt some of these men were later involved in decisions that related to those built at home.

When Britain lost Minorca again they took up a new naval base at Sicily from 1810. The island was inspected by Sir Charles Stuart. Some old Spanish towers had already been upgraded, and seven more towers were built after the island became a British base.

The danger of invasion from the French was more prevalent in Ireland than on the mainland because of the sympathy of many Irish for the French. Some believed that the French could be allies in removing the British from their country, but whether the country would have been better off under French rule is of course debatable.

The French had first tried to invade Ireland in 1796. The plan involved several waves of troops landing, to be supported by the dissident Irish. There were also to be French

Another tower commemorated on a stamp is this one from Antigua. Towers were built on many of the islands of the West Indies.

attacks on Newcastle and Bristol at the same time to divert attention from Ireland. The plan rapidly fell apart. The force that was supposed to attack Newcastle mutinied before it even arrived, while the fleet bound for Ireland was split up at sea. Despite this mishap a substantial number of soldiers, thought to be around 14,000, arrived in Bantry Bay, but they did not attempt to land as they were waiting for their commander, General Hoche, who was on one of the ships that did not arrive, and also because the weather was too bad. Bere Island in Bantry Bay was one of the sites of a later tower, perhaps owing to this attempted invasion. That forty-three French ships were able to sit in Bantry Bay for almost a month without being spotted by the Royal Navy dampened the confidence that the British public had in the Navy's ability to protect the country from invasion.

The planned attack on Bristol turned into a landing in Wales in 1797, after the attack on Ireland had already failed. The French expected that, like the Irish, the Welsh would rise up and join an invading army against the British. This army numbered less than 2,000 men, most soldiers being convicts who had been released specifically to take part in the invasion. They landed on a remote beach at Carreg Wastad Point so as not to have to fight troops at Fishguard. Rather than inspiring the locals to join

Tower Sutton was known as No. 1 Tower and was the first built in Dublin. It stands on the north coast of Dublin Bay and is now a holiday home. (Mary McGillcuddy)

them, the French turned them against their cause by burning the church at Llanwnda and by looting local homes, as well as shooting a young woman in the leg and raping her. The Welsh episode must have made dissident Irishmen wonder about the sense of supporting a French invasion of their homeland. Eventually the French Army in Wales lost heart and surrendered to British forces at Fishguard, which consisted of several groups of volunteers and assorted locals.

Despite the farcical nature of the invasion, it caused widespread panic because of the ease with which the French force had landed on the mainland. Strong action was needed by the government to reassure the population and to restore confidence in the security of Britain's shores – even if it was as expensive as building a large number of towers.

These events were followed by an Irish rebellion in 1798. This was put down after a battle at Vinegar Hill – one of the many less-than-noble actions by the British Army in Ireland. The Irish rebels numbered around 20,000, many of whom were women and children. A British artillery bombardment killed large numbers of them before the British forces moved in. As the Irish escaped through a gap in the British formation the cavalry attacked, slaughtering anyone they could, including women and children; the British troops even burnt a hospital that was caring for the wounded. These events were capitalised on by the French, who this time managed to land a force at Killala under General Humbert, fully expecting to be supported by the Irish. This invasion force was much smaller than the earlier one, only consisting of around 1,000 men, but on landing they were joined by around the same number of Irishmen. They managed to beat off two British attacks, and tried to enforce conscription on the Irish population – not an action that inspired Irish support. After a battle at Ball Na Muc they finally surrendered.

Hick's Tower at Malahide, County Dublin. One of the most elaborate roof alterations to any of the towers. (Steve Popple)

The French soldiers were treated with respect by their British captors, but the Irish who had supported them were not so lucky. They were pursued by the British and slaughtered when captured, or taken prisoner and later hanged. There seems to have been a policy of keeping the Irish under control through terror tactics.

Another French ship landed a few days later, with supplies for the invasion force and more Irishmen from France, led by James Tandy – an Irishman but also a general in the French Army. Humbert had by this time been defeated, so the force left again.

Later that year Wolfe Tone (a leading figure in the Irish independence movement) returned with another French invasion force. This time the British Navy was more successful, and intercepted and defeated the large fleet. The ship that Tone was on, the *Hoche*, was captured. After being imprisoned, Tone killed himself.

The first tower was built in Ireland in 1804 at Whiddy Island. This was some time after the attempted French invasions, but the short peace of 1802 had led to the cancellation of previous defence plans. Towers continued to be built up until the end of the Napoleonic Wars. *The Times* commented on the Irish towers in October 1804, in an article that said they were for the protection of the coast from Bray to Dublin. They were described as bombproof towers from which cannon fire could be directed at enemy ships, and also as rallying and strong points for cavalry and infantry. The towers were 40 feet in diameter, 30 feet high, circular and built from granite. In this they differed from the brick-built mainland towers. The mortar holding the blocks together was made from ground granite, lime, ash, hot wax and ox blood. Their building was supervised by Lieutenant-Colonel Benjamin Fisher and the cost was around £2,000 per tower. This was much more expensive than those built in the Channel Islands but still cheaper than the mainland towers. Several of the towers differed in design and some had furnaces to heat shot. Although seventy were planned, not all were built.

Although there may have been no attacks on the Irish towers from foreign forces during the Napoleonic Wars, attacks on them occurred at a later date. In December 1867 Fouty Tower near Queenstown was attacked by Fenians, who stole guns and ammunition from the tower.

Three towers were also built in Scotland, later than most of the English towers. The first was built in Leith in 1809 by the Corporation of Edinburgh. It should be remembered that Napoleon still had plans to invade after this date, and the English East Coast towers were built at about the same time. Two towers and a battery were built in the Orkney Islands in 1812, which had less to do with the French threat than with the outbreak of war with America that year. They were designed to protect Longhope Harbour, where British ships of the Baltic trade fleet gathered to sail in convoys of sometimes up to 100 ships. They waited in the harbour for protection from warships, but were still in danger from American privateers, which the declaration of war by America had encouraged. The impunity that the American privateers enjoyed

An old print of one of the Scottish towers. This one was built to defend Leith Harbour. The Scottish towers were to defend against American raiders as well as the French.

and the success of the French fleet in reaching Ireland both seem to point to a British lack of security, despite the Navy's efforts.

The decision to fortify Longhope Harbour was made easier because there were no other fortified harbours near the Orkneys; it was not an area that had been seen as in danger of invasion by the French. Something needed to be done quickly, so a battery was planned – to be built by the summer of 1813. Major James Smyth of the Royal Engineers was sent to plan the defences. He pointed out that a battery was unsuitable: it would easily be overcome by a small force landed from a ship if the undefended rear of the battery was attacked. Towers were thought to be superior as they were much harder to take by an attack from the land as well as from the sea.

Towers could of course be surrounded but then still had to be taken. There were rumours that the towers had escape tunnels in case the garrison was to be overrun. There have even been stories of some towers being linked to neighbouring ones by tunnels. Some evidence to support this has been found but only in a very small number of cases.

Another problem was that there were no troops or militia stationed on the Orkneys to protect a battery. The idea of a tower close by, to cover the rear of the battery, was put forward and was accepted. Eventually a second tower was planned on the opposite side of the harbour, to increase security even further. The cost was estimated at £5,000 per tower. This was more expensive than the English towers, but prices had risen and the remote location added to the expense: both materials and men had to be transported there. A further expense turned out to be the land that the towers and battery were to be built on. The landowner was a gentleman named Moodie, who said that he would be happy to let the defences be built for a nominal fee. This fee turned out to be phenomenal – £50 a year: much more than the rent paid for the sites of other towers. Eventually a fee of £40 a year was agreed. It was later discovered that the land was actually jointly owned by Moodie and the Crown, so the government was actually paying rent for using its own land.

The building of the Longhope towers was overseen by a Lieutenant Skene of the Royal Engineers. He also had a house built for himself nearby, which cost over £100. He was only allowed a building allowance of £70 for his quarters, so he had to pay the difference himself.

Opposite the mouth of the bay was the island of Flott, less than a mile away – so any ship approaching the harbour would have been well within reach of the 24-pounder guns in the towers and the battery. The Hackness Tower was close to the battery and protected its rear, while the Crossness Tower stood on the other side of the harbour mouth.

The middle of the nineteenth century led to a number of invasion scares, with the unfriendly reign of Napoleon III in France, the American Civil War, wars in Europe and Fenian threats to attack shipping. There was also the threat of new iron-clad ships, which were driven by steam and were therefore not subject to the vagaries of the weather – which meant that their guns were much more accurate. Although Britain managed to keep out of these wars there was always a danger that it might be dragged into one of the conflicts against its will. Because of this the battery at Longhope had newer and bigger guns fitted, while mountings for more modern guns were fitted in the towers; but by the time this was done the danger of invasion was over again.

The towers were used again during the First World War, when a wooden structure was added to the top of one of them. The Navy used them for signalling during the Second World War.

Grain Tower, off the Isle of Grain in the River Thames, was built in 1855. The large harbour at Milford Haven also had three towers built to protect it between 1848 and 1850. The North East Tower and the South West Tower both stood in the water at high tide, as did Grain Tower. This seems a strange decision, as the sea encroaching upon some of the old towers was the reason that they fell down. These towers, though, survived. There was another tower on Stack Rock at Milford Haven. When there was a further round of defence building a few years later, and the Palmerston forts began to appear everywhere, one was planned for Stack Rock: the tower already there was incorporated into it. This reversed the usual method of strengthening older defences with new towers.

Several towers were built around the world in British colonies. For example, in 1805 a tower was built on Wansey Hill in Sierra Leone; the area later became known as Tower Hill. Between 1804 and 1806 a tower was built at Hambantota Harbour on the island of Ceylon, now Sri Lanka. When the British took Mauritius in 1810 there were a large number of French settlers still on the island. Britain was about to ban slavery and it was felt that there could be trouble from the French plantation owners, who still owned slaves. By 1829 five towers had been built to combat this threat.

Several towers were built in other parts of the empire, often to reinforce older defences. They included those on some of the islands in the West Indies, such as

Grain Tower was built much later than the other towers, in 1855. It was to defend the entrance to the River Medway from the Thames. It has been updated during other conflicts. (Steve Popple)

Tortola, the largest of the British Virgin Islands. The tower there was attached to a defence known as Fort Recovery, which was rebuilt during the Napoleonic Wars and was known locally as Tower Fort. In 1801 a tower was built above Port of Spain in Trinidad and named after General Proctor, one of the heroes of Waterloo. Another tower was built at Barbuda, attached to an old fort probably built by the Spanish near Codrington to protect the south-west of the island. Barbuda was leased by a plantation owner named Sir William Codrington, who built the tower himself: it is, I believe, the only privately built Martello tower, although other defences have been built privately such as that already mentioned on the Channel Islands.

In Jamaica a tower was built at Kingston Harbour between 1808 and 1811. A tower was also built on Bermuda at Ferry Reach in the 1820s, to protect the long channel between St George's and St David's islands. There was also a tower in Jamaica at Fort Nugent. More towers were built in Mauritius (Tamarin), Sierra Leone (Freetown) and Sri Lanka (Hambantota).

A number of towers were built in India. When the British first took Delhi in the early nineteenth century the town was surrounded by a mud wall. This was replaced with a stronger stone wall, into which were incorporated seven towers. The building of these towers was criticised later in *The Times* during the Indian Mutiny of 1857. It was argued that it was stupid to maintain a fortified town such as Delhi with 6 miles of walls and Martello towers while it held 200,000 enemies of the British.

Sixteen towers were built in Canada. The first was constructed in 1796 in Nova Scotia. This was called the Prince of Wales Tower, after Edward, son of George III, who was commanding the British forces there at the time. The late eighteenth century saw three more built: two of them in 1798 and both with royal names, the Duke of York and Duke of Clarence (after two more of George III's many male offspring). Between 1810 and 1815 four towers were built in Quebec and two in Nova Scotia. More were built in 1846 at Kingston, near Lake Ontario: four large and two small. Another was built at New Brunswick. All the Canadian towers were built during periods of threat from either France or the United States. The weather had an effect on their design: because of the threat of heavy snow many of them had a roof.

A tower was built in Corfu in 1839 when the British had a base there, and when they left the island in 1864 they blew it up. Another tower was built in South Africa in 1846, because of the prolonged trouble with the Boers.

There was even a tower built in Australia as late as the 1850s, on an island in Sydney Harbour. There were already defences there, named Fort Denison – built after seven American ships arrived unexpectedly in the harbour in 1839. The island had previously been used as a punishment area for the early convicts who were transported to Australia. The Martello tower was added, along with barracks, to increase protection against the Russian Navy during the Crimean War, and at first was manned by volunteers. It was one of the few Martello towers to face enemy action during the Second World War, when it was fired on by a ship in the harbour which was aiming at a Japanese submarine.

During the Crimean War the British had to attack towers. In July 1854 they took the forts at Bomarsund, in the Baltic, which included three large towers. The exchange of fire between these towers and British ships was recorded by an officer on board the

One of the five towers built at Halifax, Nova Scotia. The Canadian towers had a roof due to the heavy snowfall. I believe that this is the Prince of Wales tower, which is the oldest, built in the late eighteenth century.

The St John Tower, New Brunswick. This was a later tower, built in 1813.

Blenheim. There were three Martello towers in commanding positions, which fired on the *Edinburgh* and the *Amphion*. The garrison of the defences at Bomersund were eventually taken and ended up as prisoners of war back in England. Martello towers were also being built to protect Sebastopol, but the British arrived and took the area before they were completed.

The Napoleonic War led to serious problems between Britain and America which led to the building of Martello-type towers as part of the American coastal defences. The towers varied in design, some being similar to the Canadian towers, others more like the English ones.

The first was built at Dumplings Rocks in Rhode Island between 1800 and 1802 and held eight guns. There was a gap of seven years before the next tower was built at Fort Washington in Maryland. When the fort was demolished there were plans to build two new towers in the new fort but they were never built.

The next round of tower building took place during the war of 1812. There were three towers built at Walbach, New Hampshire; Tybee Island near Savannah, Georgia; and James Island, Charleston, South Carolina.

There was another built in 1829, Dupree Tower at Bayou Dupree, Louisiana, followed by three more which were larger than normal Martello towers. One was at Proctor's Landing, Lake Borne, in 1856. This was followed by two more at Key West in 1862.

There had been a number of other towers built in America between 1820 and 1835 but these were unlike the others built inland.

The Shoal Tower was one of four built in the 1840s in Kingston, Ontario.

2

THE MAINLAND

When a French invasion was first threatened, the British regular army was small and could not compare in strength with the forces massed across the Channel. Most of the available British forces were poorly trained militia and these were often unarmed, apart from those with pitchforks and pikes. The regular forces gathered together in large summer camps at strategic points around the south-east of the country. These camps had been regular summer events for many years and in many cases had become tourist attractions, with large crowds coming to watch the sham battles that the troops put on. These camps were often criticised by the press, being seen as an excuse for gentlemen to play at being soldiers. Officers' balls often seem to have been more important than training. Before the war with Napoleon there were only summer camps, as there were very few barracks: until this time barracks had only been used in places such as Ireland, where a large number of troops were needed to keep order. Historically the government had not wanted large forces of soldiers gathered together in one place, in case this threatened their authority. Troops were normally housed in tents, and this could only happen in the warmer months. War was mainly a summer occupation. During the winter regular forces were often billeted in inns. The Napoleonic Wars changed this situation: there was an urgent need for a larger army and for somewhere for the troops to live.

Another reason for the building of barracks was that innkeepers were getting fed up with being overrun by the soldiers who were billeted on them. Often there was no room at inns for members of the public, as they were catering for so many soldiers – and this was a great inconvenience for travellers.

The country was divided into twelve military districts. Relevant to this book are the Eastern District (Norfolk, Suffolk and Essex) and the Southern District (Kent and Sussex). Each district had an officer in command who during the French wars had to carry out a survey of coastal defences, working with an officer from the Royal Engineers.

The barrier against invasion by Napoleon was based on three forms of defence. First there was the Navy, which controlled the seas around the coast and was probably the most important element in the fight against the French forces. As we have already seen, this might not have been as effective as generally assumed. Second there were the troops (regulars, militia and volunteers) who would fight the invading forces if they managed to land on British soil. Finally there were fortifications, which included batteries and defensive structures. These were mainly from earlier periods, and only a few were built specifically for this war – during the early years of the conflict. These were mainly batteries.

The Hythe School of Musketry was the site of a number of towers. There are still ranges on the site but not all the towers have survived.

Coastal defences suffered from a serious lack of manpower, and the increase in the number of batteries in 1797 made this shortage even more acute. The volunteer units that sprang up around the country during the war were almost entirely infantry and cavalry. To combat this, many of the volunteers in coastal areas were only given enough muskets for a third of their strength – in order to encourage them to train on the large guns that already existed in their areas.

During the short peace of 1802–03 all the volunteer units were disbanded and guns were removed from many batteries. This was obviously a premature move. When the war began again in 1803 the War Office posted a few permanent staff to the newly reformed volunteer units. This developed into a scheme in mid-century when 450 invalid gunners were posted to coastal districts as master gunners. They were supported by local volunteer district gunners, whom they trained to man coastal defences.

In 1795 a series of signal towers was established on the mainland. There were thirty towers listed in *The Times* in September 1795, a list which not only gave the position of the towers but also included the name of the lieutenant commanding each new post. Each tower had a staff of a lieutenant, a midshipman and two seamen. The system of signalling became so well developed that messages could be passed from the South Coast to London very quickly, thereby informing those in the capital of an invasion soon after it happened.

The early threat of invasion was removed when Napoleon decided to take his army to Egypt instead. This gave Britain time to prepare for the danger in case it recurred, but the Peace of Amiens in March 1802 put an end to this, and the militia and much of the regular army were disbanded. This was welcomed by the public, who had to pay for the large army through higher taxes.

Shorncliffe Camp was one of a number of military sites on the Kent coast. As well as barracks there were a number of towers on the site as well.

This short period of peace with the French was not seen as permanent by the politicians, so preparation for future conflict did not stop altogether. One of Britain's most successful soldiers, John Moore, was given the opportunity to train a new force: the light infantry. Moore had been in the Army since the age of fifteen and had a vast amount of experience. He had been based in Minorca and saw action in America during the Revolution, by which time he was a lieutenant. He became an MP, but in 1787 was promoted to major. Moore also fought in Corsica, and was later posted to the West Indies. In 1798 he became a major-general, then served in Ireland during the rebellion of 1798. Here he was one of the more humane commanders, at a time when atrocities committed by the British Army were quite common. After leaving Ireland he was put in charge of the defence of part of the South Coast. During this time he trained his new light infantry, which was recognised as the most reliable unit in the British Army.

Much of the training of Moore's light infantry took place at Shorncliffe Camp on the Kent coast, which put him in a strong position to play a major part in coastal defence when the war began again and Napoleon assembled an enormous army across the Channel. There were rumours of a planned tunnel under the Channel or even balloons above it, but the obvious and conventional plan for invasion was to use boats.

In 1803 Moore was commander of the Southern District. He disagreed with government policy in the event of an invasion, which was to harry the invaders until larger forces could be sent against them. Moore wanted to force the invasion force into an instant all-out battle on the beaches.

At this time William Pitt the Younger was Warden of the Cinque Ports and living at nearby Walmer Castle. He played a large part in training the reformed local militia, and hoped to lead them to fight alongside Moore if the invasion came. Pitt was disappointed with Moore's plan – which was to have the militia watching from high ground while his regulars fought the French on the beaches.

The volunteers that had been disbanded during the short peace had mainly been privately raised by local gentlemen. When the war began again the volunteers were financed by the government, being paid for eighty-five days of service in their local area and for another twenty days if they would serve anywhere in the country. It was often necessary to send volunteers to other areas to quell local disturbances. This was so that they were not asked to fire on their own neighbours – and, of course, there was doubt that they would obey such an order.

The French invasion plan was simple: hundreds of small boats were being built to carry a large force across the Channel. The British knew this because one of the French officers who had been involved in earlier invasion plans, General Dumouriez, had defected to Britain, and was able to advise on France's most likely course of action.

Plans for Martello towers now came to the fore. The normal explanation, as mentioned above, is that those in positions of responsibility who had been at the attack on the Corsican tower influenced the decision to build them. An example is General Sir David Dundas, who was commander of the Southern District between 1803 and 1805, and had been in Corsica during the Mortella Point battle. This explanation may be partly true, but as the towers in the Channel Islands were built before the Mortella incident the explanation is probably not as simple as it might seem; there may have been other reasons. In 1776 the Marquis de Montalembert had put forward the view that the best form of coastal defence was a high, bombproof tower. De Montalembert was a French officer who had become an expert in fortification and published a book on the subject. After the Revolution he spent some time living in England, so his views may have been known among the military hierarchy. It may well be that his work inspired the building of towers in Britain and its colonies before the Mortella Point incident occurred. However, in the second half of the eighteenth century military engineers usually built defences that best suited individual circumstances – so it may just have been common knowledge that towers were the best form of coastal defence, and the Mortella incident merely provided a practical illustration of this theory. Another factor was cost: towers were cheaper than batteries and therefore more of them could be built, protecting more of the coast.

In 1797 Dundas had stated that strong stone towers garrisoned by around thirty men were a better form of coastal defence than batteries, because batteries were more vulnerable to an attack from a land-based force. I have not found any examples of a battery on the British mainland being taken by an enemy force, but French batteries were often taken by British seamen by landing a force that attacked from the rear. A letter from Captain, later Admiral, Lord Cochrane written in May 1806 describes just such an incident. Lieutenant Norton of the cutter *Frisk* and Lieutenant Gregory of the gun brig *Contest* went ashore to flank the battery at Point d'Equillon and to attack it from the rear. The fifty men manning the battery were put to flight and the three 36-pounder guns were spiked. The battery and barracks were then blown up.

Having served the Duke of York in the Seven Years' War, Dundas had a big influence on the commander-in-chief and he was the commander of the Southern District. This and the Eastern district, under Sir James Craig, were the two most vulnerable of the twelve military districts, so it is no surprise that it was in these areas that the most thorough defences were built.

In 1798 a Major Reynolds had put forward a plan for the building of 143 towers between Littlehampton and Yarmouth. Of this number he believed that seventy-three were urgently needed, forty-eight were necessary and twenty-two were desirable. While the Irish towers were being planned, we know that a similar strategy was being discussed for the South and East Coasts of England. Colonel Twiss had advised the Duke of York in 1803 of the advantages of strong coastal defences, and in the same year Captain W. H. Ford, who was stationed at Shorncliffe Camp and on Twiss's staff, sent the General of Fortification, General Morse, plans for square towers costing £3,000 each. Ford favoured square towers as they could hold more guns than round ones. He had been in Minorca where there were both old watchtowers and towers built by the British, and had also been at Mortella – where the tower was round. Ford had the ear of the Prime Minister, Henry Addington, who was a personal friend. Twiss disagreed with Ford, however, saying that round Martellos were preferable and would cost only £2,000 each. Twiss had been in America and Canada, where towers were also built, and later became a brigadier-general and governor of the Royal Military Academy at Woolwich. This was where tests were carried out on the suitable thickness of tower walls.

Therefore the idea of building coastal towers had been around since before the Peace of Amiens. Although the Duke of York as commander-in-chief later accepted Ford's

An old postcard of the beach at Hythe, showing one of the towers there.

plans, nothing more was done – as the plans were bogged down in endless political committees. It may seem strange that a mere captain such as Ford had such an influence on major decisions, especially as the Royal Engineers had a strength of less than 200 men early in the war. However, an engineer was posted at all bases at home and abroad and was responsible for building military constructions such as barracks. They were important members of the officers' ranks, and although they were not always senior officers they had a great deal of influence.

William Pitt the Younger became Prime Minister again on 10 May 1804 and within days, on 18 May, Napoleon installed himself as Emperor of France. Pitt, it seems, was also in favour of building the towers and his return as Prime Minister was enough to sway the balance – especially as the Duke of York was in favour of towers as well. In the same year a defence committee was formed, which included six members who had been involved in the attack on the tower in Corsica: Colonel D'Aubant, Major-General Dundas, Rear-Admiral Elphinstone, Vice-Admiral Sir John Jervis, later Lord St Vincent, Lieutenant-Colonel John Moore and Lieutenant-Colonel Nepean.

Colonel John Brown inspected the defences on the South Coast in 1804 and sent his findings to Dundas. His view was that the existing batteries were too few and too far apart to be of any use at all in stopping an invasion force. Brown had been responsible for building batteries in Ireland, which had as good as fallen down soon afterwards – witnessed by Moore while he was serving there. Despite this earlier failure, however, Brown's new idea was accepted by the Duke of York: a military canal that stretched through Kent into Sussex, making Romney Marsh – one of the areas most vulnerable to invasion by the French – into an island. This meant that an earlier plan to flood the Marsh in the event of an invasion could be abandoned. Flooding Romney Marsh would have brought with it several problems, among them being that it could have taken up to three tides to submerge the whole area, too slow to seriously hamper an invasion force; and the flood would have ruined the land for some time afterwards. If there had been a false alarm it would have been a very expensive mistake. Colonel Brown's idea for a canal, put forward to the lords of the Marsh in September 1804 at a meeting at New Hall in Dymchurch, by Pitt, Moore and Twiss, was therefore very popular. A report in the *Sussex Chronicle* stated that there would be a rampart on the north side, protecting a military road with batteries. Vessels of up to 200 tons would be able to navigate the waterway. This plan for the Royal Military Canal was accepted and it eventually stretched for 30 miles, from Hythe in Kent to Rye in Sussex.

Also in 1804 Twiss carried out a further survey of the Kent and Sussex coasts, to decide exactly where the towers should be placed. Although Brown was against the idea of towers because of the expense, these plans were also approved. John Rennie was employed as the canal's consultant engineer and there was an influx of labourers to build both the canal and the towers. Although Pitt had been popular in Kent while he lived there, many more suspicious persons held the view that his plan for increased work in the area was the real reason for his popularity.

The defence scheme was finally agreed upon, and work began on the canal and the towers together with defences on the Western Heights above Dover. It was to be 1808 before the towers were completed, forming a line of defences that were strengthened by several other batteries and defences already in existence.

One of the towers at Dymchurch from a postcard from the early twentieth century.

The French plan to invade Britain involved the use of the French Navy, which for much of the war was blockaded in port by the British. Napoleon's plan was for the French ships to escape from the blockade and lead the British ships off to the West Indies, by threatening their possessions there. Giving the British the slip, they would return to the Channel and assist in the invasion together with hundreds of smaller boats. Many of the smaller boats that had been built to carry the army were no more than glorified rafts, and their stability was suspect. Napoleon was no sailor and did not really understand naval matters. The numbers involved in the plan were around 150,000 men and 10,000 horses – more of which could have been acquired after landing in England. What was needed was very calm weather for the unseaworthy boats. The plan failed completely, much to Napoleon's disgust.

The danger of imminent invasion passed in October 1805, when a Franco-Spanish fleet under Admiral Villeneuve was defeated at the Battle of Trafalgar: never again would Napoleon have the chance to challenge the British at sea. At this point Napoleon changed his mind about invading England, took his army away from the Channel coast and headed for Austria instead. With the danger passed, Moore took command of British forces in Portugal, where he died at the hands of a vastly superior French Army at the Battle of Corunna in January 1809. Although Moore was criticised at the time, he is now generally recognised as one of the most outstanding commanders of the period.

Despite the removal of French forces from across the Channel, the danger of invasion did not entirely disappear. It must be remembered that Napoleon controlled most of Europe by this time. Although many argue that the Battle of Trafalgar in 1805 spelt the end of French invasion plans, because of the number of ships that were lost, new ships were constantly being added to the French Navy. The rebirth of Napoleon's plan could not be ruled out, despite the major setback. The Walcheren expedition of 1809 was intended to destroy the French fleet at Flushing, which indicates that French naval power had not entirely been broken by Trafalgar – and it was not until Napoleon's disastrous invasion of Russia in 1812 that the danger of invasion was finally over. For obvious reasons, therefore, the building of coastal towers continued after Trafalgar – but whatever the rights and wrongs of the building of the towers, and the timing of this, they were never called upon to participate in a battle with the French.

When the war ended most of the towers were only occupied by one man, who was employed to keep them in good condition. Owing to their often remote positions, it was a constant worry that if the man in the tower became ill he would not be found. To combat this a number of towers were shut up, and two men were put in each of the others – so they had support. It was soon found that when they were shut the towers quickly began to deteriorate, which is surprising when one considers how strongly built they were. As a solution, invalid soldiers were put into them, either sappers or miners, just to keep the buildings aired. As money became short many of the towers became the responsibility of local barrack-masters instead of the War Office.

The towers attracted a great deal of criticism almost immediately, and were also often unrecognised for what they were. One of their biggest critics was the soldier, writer and politician William Cobbett. In his *Rural Rides* written in 1820 he described his first sight of the towers along the coast between Dymchurch and Hythe in Kent. He saw a great round building standing on the beach and had scarcely time to wonder what it could be before seeing twenty to thirty more along the coast. Cobbett described the towers, sarcastically, as monuments to the wisdom of Pitt, Dundas and Percival. His main criticism seemed to be the cost, which he guessed as between £5,000 and £10,000 each – and one had recently been sold in Sussex for only £200.

Cobbett was not a fan of any of the defences that had been constructed along the South Coast to deter Napoleon. He criticised the number of barracks near Hythe and the Royal Military Canal. He seemed to have a valid point of view: as he said, Napoleon's forces had been used to crossing the Rhine and the Danube, and would already have crossed the Channel when they had arrived at the canal – so a waterway that was 30 feet wide would hardly deter them. However, Cobbett's criticisms of the Martello towers seem to have been made with the benefit of hindsight. When they were built there was a real danger of invasion, and if this had occurred the towers would have played a major role in the defence of the country. If a French attack had been driven off successfully they would have been worth every penny.

Cobbett had an innate dislike of the military authorities, and his complaints should be taken in the context of his disapproval of all things military – and also his critical nature. After starting life as a farm labourer he had joined the Army, and by his own hard work he had become a regimental clerk and then sergeant-major in the 54th Regiment of Foot. In his later writing he was very critical of the standard of Army officers, and described his own work as telling the officers what to do. After leaving the Army he accused a number of officers of stealing the pay of the enlisted men, and had to flee to France to escape the consequences. He was later jailed, and spent two years in prison for his opposition to flogging in the Army.

There was an interesting connection between Cobbett and one of the naval heroes of the war, Captain Lord Cochrane, who was also MP for Westminster. Cochrane tried to combat the abuses of the prize system and the fortunes made by the men in charge of the Admiralty, while those who did the fighting earned much less. He was also annoyed at tracts that were sent to the officers of ships, which he refused to circulate to the men, as he believed that they caused divisions between them. He sent some of them to Cobbett, and the resulting publicity that Cobbett aroused led to some animosity against Cochrane for his actions.

Cobbett's criticism of the towers on the grounds of expense must have been viewed sympathetically by Cochrane. His father had been an inventor and had tried to persuade the Admiralty to use coal tar to protect the bottom of warships from rotting. This was in the days before copper sheathing was used, and it would have undoubtedly been a money-saving exercise. The Admiralty refused to contemplate the idea, and when he attempted to apply the idea to merchant shipping he was told by shipbuilders that the quicker ships rotted the better, as it gave them more work.

There has been more criticism of the towers since Cobbett's day. Writing in the 1930s, Kenneth Walker said that 'we can take no pride in the reminders of a time of fear and a costly mistake by the government'. Once again, would that criticism have stood if Napoleon had invaded and the towers had been successful in deterring him? However, not everyone is critical of the construction of the towers and the canal. Writing in *The Hammers of Invicta* (1981), I. Glendenning wrote that the government must have been happy to be able to build such strong coastal defences for around £500,000 – and certainly when the expense of building warships is considered, the cost of a tower seems reasonable. Nelson's flagship the *Victory* had cost nearly £60,000 when it was built in 1765. Taking into account the rising prices during the war, how many ships could have been built for the same price as the towers? Would a few extra ships have been as strong a deterrent to invasion? Added to this, there is always a danger that expensive ships can sink before they play any major part in a war, and yet criticism of their construction is rare.

It is also important to take into account the fears of the British population regarding a French invasion. The French Army were not known for their kind treatment of conquered populations, and the thought of Napoleon struck fear into the hearts of many. When the French landed not only in Ireland but also on the mainland in Wales, a French conquest of England seemed all the more likely. A contemporary view was expressed by J. C. Shenstone: 'For many years those living near the East Coast were inspired with great terror lest this invasion should take place. Older friends often recounted the nights that they spent in fear and trembling when false reports arrived of the landing of the enemy.'

The danger of invasion was seen as so real that plans were made to evacuate the royal family from London to Worcester, although the king planned to play a part in the defence of the country and wanted to lead the army himself. He planned to move to Chelmsford to set up a government if the invasion was on the Essex coast or to Dartmouth if it was in Kent.

The Martello tower at Alderburgh in Suffolk. This was different in design to all the other towers in being a triple tower.

The threat that Napoleon (the 'Bogeyman') would come to get you was commonly used by parents to subdue their children – 'Bogeyman' deriving from Bonaparte. Rumours of secret French landings were common. Some embedded themselves in local consciousness as truth rather than fiction, and when Thomas Hardy told a tale about Napoleon landing in Dorset to survey the countryside this was based on local folklore. If the building of towers had the effect of calming the nerves of the population, would that not have been worth the expense?

What critics of the towers seem to forget is the vast amount of money that Britain paid to her allies to help them in their fight against the French. By bankrolling the wars of foreign powers, Britain hoped to keep the French occupied on the Continent. In relation to this expense, which in many cases was not particularly cost-effective, the towers were relatively cheap and a greater deterrent.

The Industrial Revolution and opportunities for worldwide trade in the growing empire put Britain in a very strong financial position at the outbreak of war. A point made by Cobbett is that the common people in most cases did not share in this new-found wealth. Would they have been better off if the government had saved the money that was spent on towers? Obviously not: the wages of those involved in erecting the towers and building the canal helped the poor more than any other aspect of the war.

Despite Cobbett's view, the building of Martello towers was to continue in Britain for many years after the end of the Napoleonic Wars – as mentioned above. Although they may not have been used in the war against the French, they played a part in a serious conflict between the English and government forces: the fight against smuggling.

Smuggling had been a recognised problem in England since the thirteenth century, following the imposition of customs duties by Edward I. During the French Revolution French aristocrats in danger of the guillotine found refuge in Britain with the aid of British smugglers who carried them to safety. This worked in reverse: if they had the money French prisoners in England could always find a smuggler willing to return them to France. A smuggling gang in Whitstable specialised in this trade above any other goods. A little later, much of the gold used to pay French troops during the Napoleonic Wars came from Britain. Gold guineas were taken across the Channel by smugglers acting on behalf of bankers in London, who made huge profits from the practice – as a guinea in France was worth 9s more than in England.

Smuggling, however, became more difficult during the Napoleonic Wars. The building of so many new defences, signal stations and barracks along the coast meant that arrivals were more closely watched – and although the French were the target, native smugglers arriving on the beaches were just as likely to be seen.

British smugglers landing in France were not as fiercely resisted as one might imagine. It is said that much of Napoleon's intelligence from Britain came via British smugglers, and for this reason he encouraged them to visit France, even allowing large groups to inhabit some parts of the country permanently. However, there is some dispute over this. For example, the *Chelmsford Chronicle* reported in November 1810 that a decree had been made by Napoleon. Directed at English smugglers, it threatened them with a long prison sentence and branding on the forehead, while all English goods found in France or any territories occupied by the French were to be burnt.

When the Napoleonic Wars ended and the towers seemed to be surplus to requirements, Captain Hanchet, chief of the Preventive Waterguard (founded in 1809), whose job it was to stop smuggling, contacted the Ordnance Board and asked if the towers could be used by his men. There were a number of unconnected groups involved in the suppression of smuggling at this time. As well as the Waterguard there were the Riding Officers, the Customs and the Coastguard. Far from working together, these groups often hindered each other in their work. In 1822 a commission was set up to discuss this problem, and it was decided that the Preventive Waterguard would be the primary organisation. A change in its duties meant that this was the beginning of what we know as the Coastguard.

The Preventive Waterguard was later replaced in some areas by the Coastal Blockade service. This only operated in Kent and Sussex and existed for just a short period after the Napoleonic Wars, despite being probably the most effective way of combating smuggling. The Coastguard became active in other areas, and eventually took over from the Coastal Blockade in 1831.

Smuggling by large gangs, which either evaded the coastal forces or fought them off by strength of numbers, was mainly over by the time the war began – but not entirely. Post-war smugglers were likely to be more cunning and less open than their predecessors. Those that turned to violence to carry on their trade were likely to be ex-members of the forces, and there were even reports of smuggling gangs being trained how to fight by ex-soldiers. The poor state of the economy after the war was one reason why many men turned to smuggling; they often had little choice. The trade was an accepted way of life for those living near the coast, and smuggled goods were

The defences at Sheerness Dockyard range from various dates. These include a later Martello-type tower that was not one of the numbered towers of the Kent coast.

purchased in all levels of society. The most violent and worst-affected areas were on the South Coast, which was why the Coastal Blockade was set up there.

The Coastal Blockade was first suggested by Captain William McCulloch, or 'Flogging Joey' as he was known. The nickname points to his nature, and there were a number of floggings of his men – as even those Coastal Blockade men who worked on shore came under naval law. The modern idea of a flogging captain is probably influenced by the portrayal of such men as Captain Bligh in *Mutiny On The Bounty*. However, such punishment was quite commonplace, and accepted by many as a vital part of naval discipline. In his 1831 account of the practice Captain W. N. Glascock states, 'In the envy displayed by our enemies towards our excellent institutions there is none more insidious or to be more dreaded than the proposal to abrogate the practice of inflicting corporal punishment in the Navy. This is to awaken the most lively sympathy in those who in ignorance of the service and the difficulty of preserving discipline aboard can never be qualified to assume the office of umpire.' He went on to state that during the naval mutinies at Spithead and the Nore, which took place during the French wars, severe corporal punishment was used by the mutineers to maintain order, despite the officers having been sent off the ships. Glascock also had much to say on the Coastal Blockade itself, including this interesting detail of the service's operation: 'When on duty all intercourse or even ordinary communication with either stranger or acquaintances is strictly forbidden, even when off duty the men are interdicted from all communication with neighbouring inhabitants and from entering a public house.'

Captain McCulloch was given the command of HMS *Ganymede* in 1815, and his job was to prevent smuggling. He was a man who put his heart into anything he did, and the Coastal Blockade was his idea. He became its first commander, and after he died in 1824 he was succeeded by Captain Hugh Pigot. The first area to be covered was between Dover and Margate, in 1817. It later extended to cover all of Kent and Sussex, with McCulloch directing operations from his man-of-war HMS *Ramilies*, moored off Deal. At first the Blockade operated from ships; later, though, Martello towers were used as shore stations, in some cases being taken over from the Preventive Waterguard. There were often three families to a tower: married men based on shore were allowed to take their wives with them. This use of the towers was allowed by the Ordnance Board, which no doubt was glad to get some of them off its hands – although it still owned them. Not everyone agreed with the decision, as it was felt that a condition for using the towers should be responsibility for their upkeep. It was not only towers that were put to use: a number of the remaining coastal forts and batteries were shared between the Coastal Blockade men and the Army. Other posts were constructed where there were none suitable, and small naval craft were also beached in some places for use as quarters.

The Coastal Blockade men from the towers patrolled beaches night and day to try and stop the smugglers – but the problem was catching them in the act. Despite this, it is a fact that the towers saw more action from the smugglers than they ever did from French troops.

Although press gangs had stopped working in 1815, one of the punishments for smuggling was impressment into the Navy for five years. The problem for McCulloch was that smuggling was so ingrained into the local culture that it was the Blockade men who were often seen to be the ones causing the problems. Local magistrates were loath to convict smugglers, and a number of Blockade men found themselves on charges of assault or even murder when they used force to do their job or when they were protecting themselves from attack. There were also problems because customs officers were able to overrule the Blockade men.

Living in the Martello towers at this time must have been quite difficult. The blockade party in the towers normally consisted of a lieutenant, two petty officers and up to ten men. The basement of the tower, reached by a trapdoor, was where the men, and women if any, slept in hammocks, married couples divided from the rest of the men by curtains. The entrance to the tower was above the ground and often reached by ladder. It is difficult to imagine how a family with children coped with these conditions.

One memory indicates how difficult living in the towers must have been. Captain J. Boteler of the Royal Navy was in Bexhill during the days of the Coastal Blockade, looking for a man named Norcott who was based in one of the local towers. He records that he met the man's wife, who said to him that she had two fears: rats and stepladders. She lived in a tower that contained both.

As well as the towers, a number of ships were part of the Coastal Blockade. The HMS *Severn* (1817–23), HMS *Ramilies* (1823–30), HMS *Hyperion* (1825–31) and HMS *Talvera* (1830–31) were all stationed off the coast of Kent and Sussex. The names of all serving Blockade men appear on the ships' books, not on the stations they

An old print of a tower on the Kent coast.

were sent to. In January 1824 *The Times* reported that Captain McCulloch had forty lieutenants, three surgeons, six assistant surgeons, three pursers and 1,800 men under his command.

Finding men to serve in the Blockade wasn't easy, and a number of Irish labourers were recruited who had no experience of the Navy. Recruiting these men was easy, as many were starving in Ireland at this time. Naval pensioners were also recruited: they were allowed to keep their pension if they enlisted, as well as receiving a wage. Naval pensions were arranged by the Greenwich Hospital, and many men paid contributions while they were serving in the Navy. These men were out-pensioners, not those who actually lived in the hospital, and allowing them to keep the pension was seen as a way of making them less open to bribery.

A complaint was laid against the men of the Blockade in 1822 by the Board of Guardians for Dover, who complained that loose women were kept at the Blockade bases and often became pregnant – thereby incurring an expense for the parish. Wherever there are groups of soldiers or sailors in every conflict I have studied there have been similar claims. It seems that a large number of men being posted to any area immediately begins a panic about the morals of local women. There always seems to be a huge overestimation of the size of the problem, and the majority of cases always seem to be based on rumours. In this case, when Captain McCulloch visited the Dover Board of Guardians he found that they could give him no actual cases. This was not the entire story, however. In 1823 Midshipman Dennis Gladwell was ordered to appear at the quarter sessions at Pevensey to abide by an order for an illegitimate female child, born to Lydia Warrener, a single woman of Pevensey, at Tower 59 on 5 September 1822.

It appears that the Coastal Blockade was an unpopular organisation. In February 1831 it was described in *The Times* as the most obnoxious service in the Navy, and in *The Naval Sketch-Book* of 1825 W. N. Glascock wrote that Navy men did not want to join the Blockade as it could affect their future career prospects.

The smugglers that the Coastal Blockade had to deal with were often well organised. A report in the *Morning Chronicle* in 1826 named Captain Batts as a smuggler who regularly drilled his troops. They were said to be known to the entire Kent population and the Blockade service.

In 1831 the service was abolished, mainly as a way of saving money, and the ships HMS *Talavera* (with seventy-four guns) at the Downs and HMS *Hyperion* (forty-two guns) at Newhaven were paid off, together with 195 officers and 3,000 seamen. The duties of the Coastal Blockade were taken over by the civilian Coastguard, which was extended to cover the entire coast; the 128 Blockade stations were taken over at a quarter of the cost. Whether they were much less effective is debatable. Many of the naval lieutenants who had been in command of the Coastal Blockade stayed on as station commanders for the Coastguard, despite it being a civilian organisation.

Not all the towers were used by the anti-smuggling organisations. Some appear to have been maintained in their original capacity, with a number being re-armed in 1830, 32-pounder guns replacing the old 24-pounders.

The Coastguard had more to deal with than smuggling, often having to adjudicate in disputes between local and national authorities. For example, in March 1866 there was a dispute over unpaid church rates for the Coastguard stations in Dymchurch. There seem to have been no clear guidelines about whether these should have been paid, as similar disputes come up again and again. In this case, the Board of Guardians in Dymchurch had tried to collect the local rates from the Coastguard, after the solicitor of the War Department had informed the barrack-master at Shorncliffe (who controlled the towers in this area) that those in the service of the Crown were not liable for rates. Perhaps the guardians thought that the Coastguard were not exempt, like the military, as they were a civil institution – or perhaps they were just trying their luck. A series of letters passed between the concerned parties, and on 11 December 1866 a letter from the War Office, acknowledging receipt of a letter from the guardians, stated that that they had to communicate with the barrack-master at Shorncliffe before any decision could be reached. This seems to indicate that there were still no clear rules. A later letter from the barrack office at Shorncliffe stated that they were directed by the Secretary of State for War that those serving the state were not liable for rates. The argument continued, with the Board of Guardians claiming that the Coastguard were not serving the state and that the Coastguard stations were not state-owned buildings. It is not clear who they thought owned them. Eventually the barrack-master appears to have had enough of the matter, passing it back to the War Office and telling the local board that he hoped they would receive a satisfactory reply. Unfortunately that is the last letter that survives, so we don't know if the rates were ever paid.

By the 1840s possible invasion from France was once again being discussed. Iron-clad steamships were seen as having increased the danger; even a country with an inferior navy could be a danger if it possessed the much more manoeuvrable steam-powered warships, which did not depend on a favourable wind. The coast was once again surveyed and new defences recommended.

The *Illustrated London News* of 20 August 1853 reported on a new form of coastal defence that was being proposed, which involved using men who were living on the coast and employed for part of the year in fishing or agriculture as a volunteer sea militia – who would be trained to crew a number of shallow-draught steam gunboats, to be stationed where landings by enemy forces were seen as possible. The Sea Fencibles recruited during the Napoleonic Wars were very similar. There were also plans to build more on-shore batteries, so that the sea and land militia could practise firing guns. The use of existing batteries, forts and the remaining Martello towers was quite common when the new volunteer units were formed a few years later.

In 1855 the Ordnance Department was abolished and its responsibilities were taken over by the War Office. The sappers and miners were amalgamated into the Royal Engineers. Coastal defences were manned by a master gunner and volunteers who were trained by him. These defences were updated again in 1859. The arrival of iron-clad ships meant that the old solid ball shot was useless. Many of the older guns were rifled, allowing them to fire shells instead. Eventually the old guns were replaced with more modern weaponry.

The Duke of Wellington was dismissive of the use of existing towers and redoubts in the middle of the nineteenth century, when he inspected them. However, he eventually decided that they had a role to play in defending of the country although the improved weapons aboard steamships made the towers less defensible: he described them as no more than sentry boxes, and was also critical of the guns they were armed with. Experiments in which some of the new guns were fired at the towers may have disproved his views.

With the inception of the volunteer regiments in 1859 it was suggested in the *Manchester Guardian* that despite most volunteers wanting to be in the rifles, the Martello towers that still lined the coast could be occupied by artillery volunteers – who often used them for artillery practice. By 1873 many of the towers were occupied by married men of the Royal Artillery.

In the 1870s there was an interesting idea put forward that unfortunately was never put into practice. The use of gun turrets on warships was becoming common at this time, and a Lieutenant Duncan of the Royal Artillery had the idea of using similar turrets on land forts, so the guns could be brought to bear on all points. He also suggested that they should be fitted to Martello towers; although they already had this facility, the new turrets would have provided more protection for the gunners.

By the end of the nineteenth century many of the towers had already disappeared. The new century was to see threats from new enemies, and despite being outdated long before the First World War a number of the remaining towers were pressed into use once again as defensive structures. This happened again during the Second World War, when a number of the towers that had been turned to other uses were reclaimed by the forces and used again. Some had more modern defences added, such as modern guns.

3

KENT

All the towers built along the South Coast were similar in design but with several small differences. The main contractor responsible for the erection of the South Coast towers was William Hobson, and he sub-contracted the work to a number of other builders. This is why there are differences between the towers. However, they all had three floors and were 33 feet high. Each consisted of about 500,000 bricks. These South Coast towers were slightly smaller than the later ones built on the East Coast.

The ground floor or basement did not have an entrance from outside: it was reached through a trapdoor from the floor above. It was used as a storeroom for food, ammunition and so on, which was lowered in by pulley. The basement was very dark. As it was too dangerous to have naked flames near the powder in the magazine, the room was lit by a lantern in an alcove in the wall, separated from the magazine by a sheet of glass. There was a water tank in the basement which was fed by rainwater. If the tower was under siege the area would also have been used as a latrine.

The entrance to the tower was at first-floor level, about 10 feet off the ground, and was normally accessed by a ladder, which could be pulled up after the garrison had entered. A number of the towers also had protective ditches and two had moats: these were entered by a drawbridge, which could be raised and lowered from inside. The first floor was where the men's living quarters were, with a very unfair division of space between the officer and twenty-four men.

The upper gun platform or roof was accessed by a stairway built into the walls. The gun, a 24-pounder that could fire a solid shot about a mile, was mounted on a pivot that allowed it to be fired in any direction. The door had a hole in it, through which ammunition could be passed, and had to remain closed when the gun was fired. The chimney pots could be removed during action. The type of traversing platform that was used to hold the guns on the towers had been used in earlier batteries at the end of the eighteenth century. It gave a smaller number of guns a greater field of fire than if they had been set on normal gun carriages. They had a great advantage over guns on ships, as those could only be fired through gun ports in a fixed position. Aim was dependent on weather conditions and tide, giving the land-based guns even more of an advantage. A ship of seventy-two guns did not necessarily outgun a small land-based battery, as at any time on a rough sea as few as a fifth of the ship's guns could be brought to bear on a target. This evened the odds slightly.

The tower walls tapered to help deflect any cannonballs fired at them. The walls were much thicker on the side facing the sea, up to 13 feet, whereas the land-side wall was often only about 6 feet thick. This meant that the towers were oval despite looking and often being described as being round.

Although most towers were built within sight of the next, so as to provide support, there were exceptions depending on the ground. A number of the Kent towers were built in pairs rather than in long series (like those in Sussex), to defend the Royal Military Canal sluice gates.

Some interest was shown in the Kent towers by Rudyard Kipling in 1905. The well-known writer was apparently inspired in this by his young daughter. He wrote to the First Sea Lord Sir John Fisher asking if it would be possible to rent a tower in Kent as a summer home. Sir John seemed to think that the Warden of the Cinque Ports might be able to help, and passed the letter on to Sir Evan Macgregor, the Secretary of the Admiralty, requesting that he ask Sir Edward Ward, Under Secretary of the War Office, to communicate directly with Kipling. Despite the involvement of so many eminent people, Kipling never did get his summer home in a tower.

An interesting comment was made about the towers at Hythe by Commander Hilary Mead RN in 1948. He stated that a few years before the ruins of some of the towers in Hythe had been easily distinguishable, but in just twelve months the tide had washed around them and thrown what remained of their masonry and guns under a covering of shingle and sand. It appears from what Commander Mead says that the remains still had guns (or recognisable parts of them) at this time (see Tower 16). Another point that the commander made was that despite the difficulties experienced by those trying to destroy the towers, nature was able to do it in no time and with very little trouble.

Tower 1

Starting from Tower 1, there is the longest remaining run of consecutive towers out of all the East and South Coast towers. Tower 1 to Tower 9 are all still standing. Unfortunately very few of the towers in this group can be seen from the others, apart from the first three, which are all within sight of each other.

Tower 1 stands on the 200-foot-high cliffs at East Wear Bay. It was in poor condition and was listed as having defective brickwork as long ago as 1873. New armament was recommended for it, however. A new fort close by was also recommended, as an enemy taking control of the hill by the tower would have an advantage over the other two lower towers.

Despite its defects Tower 1 has survived, and when it was bought by the local council (by the 1970s) some repairs were done. One of the towers on the cliffs at Folkestone was struck by lightning during a heavy storm in July 1926, and I believe that it was this one. The lightning strike made a hole in the wall, which was described in the *Manchester Guardian* as several feet thick. The tower was unoccupied at the time and some visitors who were sheltering by the tower were unharmed.

The tower still survives and is now a residence.

Tower 1 is at Folkestone, built against the backdrop of the cliffs, and is the first of the longest run of consecutive towers still standing. It is now a residence.

Tower 2

This is also on the cliffs but about 50 feet lower than the first tower. It was the site of a violent battle between the Coastal Blockade men and smugglers in 1821. A gang of smugglers was seen by those on duty, and when the Blockade men approached the gang they were fired upon – one of them being killed and three others wounded. They were rescued by a group of Blockade men who arrived from their base at Tower 1.

The tower was described as in good condition in 1873 and new armaments were recommended. There was also a suggestion that it should be connected with Tower 1 and 3 by earthworks. This seems to go against the original idea that the towers should be close enough to support each other but also able to defend themselves independently.

There was a large landslide nearby in January 1877 after a heavy storm at Folkestone Warren: two men were killed and many injured. This landslide blocked the eastern end of the Martello Tunnel, and it was the following March before the railway line that ran through the tunnel could open again. The area must have been unstable as there was a further landslide in December 1915, causing the closure of Warren Halt station. Luckily the train coming through the Martello Tunnel at the time managed to stop.

Tower 2 was sold by the council in the 1960s and has now been converted into living accommodation; it is available to rent as a holiday home. The tower is surrounded by newer housing, and a private road runs up to it between houses on Wear Bay Road.

Tower 2 is within sight of Tower 1 and stands among modern housing on Wear Bay Road. It is also a residence.

Tower 3

Built to support the Bugle Battery, as were the two nearby towers, Tower 3 also stands on the cliffs at Copt Point. It was used by the Coastal Blockade. On one occasion there was a complaint that the tower's occupants had stolen a sheep from a local butcher – and Captain McCulloch, commander of the Blockade, could not deny the truth of this. The tower was later used by the Coastguard. In 1873 it was recommended that a battery be built near the tower and that the tower should be used as a magazine.

At the turn of the century the Finn family lived here. When a member of the family who had been born in the tower was married, the event was celebrated by firing the cannon three times and launching a large balloon. The locals thought it was a warning of an invasion.

Tower 3 was also used for some time as a golf course clubhouse, and had the word 'Golf' painted on it in large letters. This led to some very vocal complaints, even a mention in *The Times* in September 1934. It was reported that a meeting of Folkestone Town Council had been called at which Councillor Hollands had protested against the sign's removal. It seems that Lord Radnor had described it as an eyesore a few weeks earlier, saying that it could be seen from all over the town – and it had been removed. Councillor Hollands (Labour) was not happy that this had occurred just because Lord Radnor had passed an opinion, feeling that the decision should have been the council's. The general feeling appears to have been against Hollands, and the report went on to

Tower 3 stands alone on the cliff, within sight of the first two towers. It is now a museum.

say that someone had told a Major-General Younghusband that someone visiting the area from France had left Folkestone because of the sign. Perhaps this was the first occasion when a Martello tower successfully drove a Frenchman away. The mayor, Alderman Castle, said that he had moved house so he could no longer see the sign, and another councillor said he knew a man who had changed his room at a local hotel because he could see it from his window.

The tower was returned to its original defensive role late in its life and became a control centre for mines during the Second World War. It is now a museum and stands alone on top of a high grass hill, still surrounded by a golf course, with a view across the bay.

Tower 4

This is at the western end of the Leas. There is a larger gap between Tower 3 and Tower 4 because of the cliffs and the presence of a battery. Towers 4 to 9 were a close group and were all moated. Tower 4 was one of the towers that was fitted with a semaphore machine.

The tower was used by the Coastal Blockade, which was involved in a major smuggling incident here in November 1821 – reported in the *Morning Chronicle*. Although large smuggling gangs had primarily been the norm before the Napoleonic Wars, the Adlington Gang was an exception, and still a powerful organisation in Kent. When they landed a load close to Sandgate Castle, by the National School, around

Tower 4 is almost completely hidden by overgrown foliage. Many of the people I asked for directions knew nothing of the tower despite it being a short distance from where they were.

400 men were involved in the operation, mainly armed with muskets and pistols. This number was not unusual: many of the men would only have been there to carry away a small amount of the smuggled goods. Thomas Moore, a master at arms, and a group of five Blockade men attacked the gang. They were joined by four more men, three of whom were wounded before they ran out of ammunition. A Mr Shallard, master's mate at Tower 4, led his men in pursuit, but failed to find the gang. As was usually the case, the Blockade men were seriously outnumbered. Although some of the goods were recovered, none of the smugglers were captured.

The tower returned to its signalling origins during the Second World War, when it was used by the Observer Corps. It is now in the garden of a house, with a large slate water tank on the ground floor. As it is completely covered with foliage, it could easily be mistaken for a large clump of bushes. There is a low fence around it.

Sandgate Castle

Despite Sandgate Castle being a much earlier defensive structure than the towers, I have included it because work carried out here while the Martellos were being built resulted in a Martello-type tower being constructed within it. The castle was never numbered as one of the Kent towers, however.

The castle guarded the road to Folkestone, but in 1798 General Grey said that it was in a ruinous condition and not worth repairing. In 1804 Brigadier General William Twiss agreed. Even so, the castle was eventually updated – with much of its old defences being demolished and the keep being reinforced to Martello standards. The tower was re-armed in 1859, when there was once more danger from the French.

In the mid-nineteenth century the castle was used as a military prison while there were severe discipline problems at Shorncliffe Camp; the soldiers based there were causing a lot of problems in the town of Sandgate. In 1873 the interior keep was described as larger than a Martello tower, with the castle able to hold thirty men and 130 barrels of powder.

The castle has been badly damaged by the sea, and is now privately owned.

Tower 5

This stands above Sandgate Castle but is not visible from there because of the buildings that now stand between them. It is situated in the grounds of a girls' school. There were once plans to use it as the school chapel, but this never happened. One of the original copper-covered magazine doors remains inside. Tower 5 is in good condition in comparison with many of its close neighbours.

Above left: Tower 5 stands in a girls' school above Sandgate Castle. It was planned to be used as a chapel. This image taken from the north-west shows how overgrown and unused it now is. (Folkestone School for Girls)

Above right: A close-up of the tower from the north-east short-cut, showing the door. (Folkestone School for Girls)

Tower 6

Tower 6 is one of the towers that stood on Shorncliffe Camp near the officers' mess. The camp was built in 1794 and already had a redoubt, built just before the towers. During the Napoleonic Wars the camp housed the best troops in the British Army, trained by the camp commander, Sir John Moore. In 1873 the camp was mainly hutted and held 163 officers, 3,200 men and 850 horses.

A report in the *Sunday Times* of 17 May 2002 listed Tower 6 along with Tower 7 and Tower 9 as included in the sale of £700 million of Ministry of Defence property, part of a strategic defence review. The towers were to be sold for the cost of an ice cream, £1 each – but the agent expected the actual price to be much more than that, and warned that purchasers would have to prove that they had the financial backing and expertise to renovate the towers to English Heritage standard. Renovations in earlier times had been carried out with little regard to the historic importance of the towers.

The towers were described by an inspector for English Heritage as dark, always leaking water and with restricted space. They did not even have roads leading to them from the main highway. The buyer would not be allowed to alter or add to the existing windows, but might be allowed to add roof extensions.

The tower now stands outside the camp perimeter and is still derelict. It has a fence round it and the moat is still visible. In a large wooded area, Tower 6 can be reached by a footpath leading from the Corniche, off Hospital Hill. It is easier to find during the autumn or winter when the foliage is not so dense, as is the second tower along the footpath.

Tower 6 is on the outskirts of Shorncliffe Camp in a remote wooded area. It can only be reached by a secluded footpath and is derelict.

Tower 7

This tower was also on Shorncliffe Camp. It was used as a military store for some time but has since been bricked up. Now outside the perimeter of the camp, it is derelict – no one having taken the opportunity offered in 2002 to renovate it. Tower 7 can also be reached from the Corniche footpath. It is the first tower that you come to, and is covered with foliage. The moat wall is also overgrown.

Tower 8

The last of the three towers that stood on Shorncliffe Camp, Tower 8 is also outside the perimeter but unlike the other two is now a home; the moat has been converted into a garden. This tower was the most likely of the three to be sold as it stands closer to the road and is less remote than its neighbours.

Tower 9

In 1873 it was recommended that Tower 9 be connected to Shorncliffe Battery by a tunnel. It is not clear if this was ever done, but tunnels were associated with other towers.

This tower is difficult to find. It is almost opposite Temeraire Heights on the other side of Hospital Hill, but is not visible from the road until you climb the very steep hill. The growth around it makes it difficult to see clearly and it is in worse condition that its close neighbours: some of the coping stones have fallen. There may be a safer and easier route to the tower from the other side, but I didn't find it.

Tower 10

On the shore at Hythe, near the site of the Imperial Hotel, Tower 10 was demolished in the late nineteenth century when the promenade was built. Fort Twiss was nearby: this was sold to the local corporation in 1869 and materials from it were used to protect Hythe Esplanade.

Tower 11

This tower was at Hythe near Saltwood Gardens. In 1873 it was protected by the sea wall, but this did not stop it being demolished in the late nineteenth century.

Tower 12

In 1873 Tower 12 was described as being 50 yards beyond the sea wall, at the south end of Stade Street, Hythe. It was the towers further west, especially Tower 20 and Tower 21, that were in most danger. Despite its safe position the tower was demolished along with Tower 10 and Tower 11.

Above: Tower 7 is in the same wooded area as its neighbour, Tower 6, alongside Shorncliffe Camp. Also derelict and very overgrown.

Left: Tower 8 is also one of the towers that previously stood on Shorncliffe Camp, but unlike its near neighbours is now used as a residence.

Tower 9 is close to Tower 8 but much less accessible and in poorer condition. I had to climb a high bank to get to it from the Hospital Hill road.

Tower 13

Tower 13 survived the demolition of its close neighbours. It was sold by the War Department in 1906 and was converted into a house called Place Forte between the wars, before being taken over and re-used as an observation post during the Second World War. In the 1960s a number of further alterations were carried out that would not be allowed today, such as inserting large windows and making the walls thinner, to increase internal space. The architect was Ronald Ward, designer of Millbank Tower, and he made the tower his home. It was put up for sale in 2003 for £495,000.

Tower 14

This is the first of the towers on Hythe Ranges, built to support three forts that dated from the late eighteenth century, when the ranges were just barracks.

In 1825 a group of smugglers was seen close to the tower by the Blockade men who, despite help from an Army officer from the Wagon Train Barracks, were assaulted. The smugglers escaped with most of the goods.

In the mid-nineteenth century Hythe Ranges became the School of Musketry. The name is misleading, as it was founded to teach officers how to instruct their men in the use of rifles, not muskets, as rifles were much more accurate. Muskets were so inaccurate that firing practice with them was of no use.

Tower 13 stands in Hythe and has been a residence for a number of years. It stands among a row of more modern houses.

Towers 14 and 15 on Hythe Ranges. The ranges are still in use and although there is public access to the beach when the red flag flies, by the first tower, it is closed.

One of the towers from the edge of the Hythe Ranges inland.

The tower is visible from the beach, and was once used to fly the red danger flag when firing was taking place on the ranges.

Tower 15

Another tower on Hythe Ranges, it is also visible from the beach. Fort Sutherland once stood between Tower 15 and Tower 16. In 1873 the barracks at Hythe could hold thirty-six officers and 261 men, while Fort Sutherland had six guns. At this time the sea was beginning to encroach on the fort, as it was built in front of the towers. It was recommended that it continue in use as stores and barracks.

Tower 16

Now destroyed by coastal erosion, Tower 16 was also situated on Hythe Ranges. Its ruins are still visible. A local girl named Dorothy whose father worked at the School of Musketry wrote that during the First World War she heard a couple speaking in German and looking at a map in the ruins of one of the towers at Hythe. I suspect it was either this tower or one of the next two: these were all in ruins at the time while the others in Hythe were either still complete or had already been demolished. The girl reported them to the authorities, and later heard that a couple had been executed as German spies. She believed that it was these two people.

Commander Mead reported that among the ruins of the tower in 1938 were two guns.

Another view of the two towers on the ranges. These are Towers 14 and 15.

Tower 17

In 1873 it was recommended that all the towers and batteries on Hythe Ranges be maintained as stores, barracks and gun emplacements as long as there was no expense involved in saving them from the sea. Unfortunately No. 17 was destroyed by erosion. The ruins are still visible.

Tower 18

There was a large battle by Tower 18 (also on Hythe Ranges) in 1821, between Coastal Blockade men and a large group of smugglers, which occurred when a boat belonging to the smugglers was captured. The tower was eventually destroyed by erosion. The ruins are still visible but no access is allowed because of the tower's position. In 1873 there were rifle ranges between Tower 14 and Tower 18.

Tower 19

The last of the towers on Hythe Ranges, this is still visible from the beach but has been partly destroyed by coastal erosion. Fort Moncrieff once stood between Tower 19 and Tower 18. In 1873 Fort Moncrieff still held six guns, but the sea was beginning to encroach upon it. Its continued use was recommended as stores and barracks.

Unfortunately, not all the towers on the ranges have survived. Above can be seen the ruins of Tower 19. (Steve Popple)

Tower 20

This was one of a pair of towers with Tower 21, the first of three pairs built to protect sluice gates on the Royal Military Canal. It vanished early in the twentieth century.

Tower 21

Tower 20 and Tower 21 were built to defend the sluice gates at Romney Marsh. Tower 21, like its neighbour, was washed away early in the twentieth century.

Dymchurch Redoubt

The Dymchurch Redoubt was one of two redoubts built on the South Coast at the same time as the Martello towers. Another was built later at Harwich in Essex when the East Coast towers were constructed. This redoubt is known locally as Brookman's Barn, after the building that stood on the site before the defence was built.

The redoubts were used as reinforcement and supply bases for the Martello towers nearby. This one was built a little earlier than Eastbourne Redoubt and had a much more elaborate heating system, with flues that carried hot air back into living quarters. This proved expensive to build and was thus not included at Eastbourne. Another difference was that Dymchurch did not have caponiers, defences that gave a field of fire across the surrounding ditch.

An old print of the Ranges. A tower is visible in the rear. When this was drawn there must have still been a number of towers on the ranges.

Three redoubts were built at the same time as the Martello towers. This one is at Dymchurch. It is the only one still in military use and has had various alterations in later conflicts.

The redoubt held eleven 24-pounder guns. It protected the coast and the surrounding marshes, and was defended by a 20-foot ditch. It had a drawbridge for entry. In 1853 the sea wall was extended around the redoubt to protect it from the sea. This was built by the local corporation, for which the War Department paid 25s a year.

In 1873 remodelling and rearmament of the redoubt was recommended. It was described as capable of holding eight officers, 130 men and 248 barrels of powder in the magazine. It was armed with two 68-pounder and nine 32-pounder guns.

The redoubt was updated with more modern defences, such as pillboxes and machine-gun posts, during the Second World War. It is still owned by the Ministry of Defence. When I visited in 2006 the whole area was fenced off and a group of soldiers were obviously using the redoubt for some kind of exercise. This is the only example of the Martellos or redoubts built during the Napoleonic Wars still being used by the forces.

Tower 22

Tower 22 was one of a pair with Tower 23. It was used by the Coastal Blockade and was the site of a battle with smugglers in 1823. This event indicates how outnumbered the Blockade men often were by the smugglers. Two men from the tower, Midshipman Hamilton and his servant, saw a group of forty men acting suspiciously, and after being joined by a few more Blockade men they bravely attacked the large group. Prisoners were taken and a smuggler was shot and later died. It is thought he was actually shot by mistake by one of the smuggling gang rather than by the Blockade men. Despite this, Midshipman Hamilton was arrested for murder and spent weeks in Maidstone Prison before his case finally came to court. He was acquitted and praised for his bravery. The arrest of Blockade men for assault and even murder when tackling smugglers was a normal event, and knowing that this could happen must have had some influence on how rigorously they pursued smugglers.

In 1826 Lieutenant Johnson, who was based at Tower 21, spotted flashes of light and heard a pistol shot. Firing a pistol was the only way that Blockade men could raise an alarm, but unfortunately it left the firer with an unloaded weapon, unable to defend himself. When Johnson arrived near Fort Moncrieff with some other men, he found a group of smugglers bringing their load ashore and protected by about thirty men armed with muskets. This was unusual, as those protecting the smugglers usually carried large sticks. The Blockade men got the worst of the fight until reinforcements arrived, and the smugglers escaped except for one wounded man. It turned out that this was the famous Adlington Gang once again.

It was recommended that the tower be re-armed with a rifled gun in 1873. It was eventually demolished by Kent County Council in 1956, to allow road-widening. The company tasked with the job had to call in the Army to blow it up, as they were unable to knock it down.

Tower 23

This was built to defend the Willop Sluice in Hythe Road, Dymchurch. At one time a family named Carr (parents and five children) lived here; it would seem that they

Tower 23 at Dymchurch is now a residence.

previously lived in Tower 24. Despite its being used as a residence, it was recommended that the tower be re-armed with a rifled gun in 1873. Restored in the 1970s, Tower 23 was being lived in by the 1990s. It sold for £850,000 in 2004.

Tower 24

Tower 24 and Tower 25 were built to guard sluice gates. According to the 1841 census Gustav Baker lived here, with George Maddock, Francis Barnes, Georgina Barnes and Henrietta Elliot. As with Tower 23, despite it being occupied in the mid-nineteenth century it was recommended that it be re-armed with a rifled gun in 1873. The tower has now been restored and is open to the public as a museum run by English Heritage, the only museum dedicated to the history of the Martello towers. It still has its gun *in situ*.

Tower 25

This tower defended the Marshland Sluice along with Tower 24. It was recommended that it be re-armed with a rifled gun in 1873. The tower was partly restored at the same time as Tower 24, but it is now unused and stands in a car park.

The tower was the scene of a fire in August 2004. Four fire engines were called, and it appeared that a pile of rubbish inside had caught fire. Witnesses said that the building looked like a large chimney with smoke coming out of it.

Above left: Tower 24 is surrounded by houses. It is now a museum and still has a cannon on the roof.

Above right: Tower 25 is also in Dymchurch but is unused and stands in a car park.

Tower 26

One of a pair with Tower 27 at St Mary's Bay, it was built to guard the sluice gates at Globsden Gut, close to the church of St Mary's. The sea was washing at its base at high tide as early as 1870. It was demolished in 1871.

Tower 27

Built to guard the Globsden Gut sluice gates with Tower 26, this was one of the towers also used as a semaphore station. In 1826 Lieutenant Cole of the Coastal Blockade, based at this tower, was at sea when he saw a ship being unloaded. The ship was seized, and one Blockade man was left on board to guard it while the others went ashore to try and catch the gang who had been unloading. Other boats arrived, and after a running battle the Blockade men returned to the seized ship to find that the guard they had set was missing. He had been murdered, and his body was found the next day.

The tower was demolished in the mid-nineteenth century.

4

SUSSEX

During the French wars of the late eighteenth and early nineteenth centuries there seem to have been surveys of the coast of Sussex to examine defences every few years. An early one was carried out by Thomas Yeakell and William Gardener in the late 1780s. This topographical survey named all the parishes, hamlets and farms in the county, and also noted the depth of water at certain points along the coast – an important factor when considering possible invasion. In 1808 Richard Searle, the royal military surveyor and draughtsman, surveyed defences on the coast near Eastbourne on the orders of Major-General Twiss. In 1812 Yeakell and Gardener's survey was used by Captain Gossett, who added all the batteries in Sussex to it.

Although there were plans in place to evacuate local people in the event of an invasion, not everyone left the details to the government. Dr John Lettice, the vicar of Peasemarsh in Sussex, issued his own plan for evacuation, as he believed that government plans would lead to confusion and panic, as individuals did not know what they were supposed to do. He organised every parish so that everyone knew what their job would be when the invasion came. Everyone was told if they would walk or ride in carts when they were evacuated. The head of every family was to go to the parish church with a blanket, all the food he had, a sack, a saucepan, a kettle and knives and forks. All livestock was to be driven with the column, and regular roll calls were to be organised. The vicar's plan was more detailed than the government's, but fortunately never had to be used.

The Times reported in March 1805 that the only part of the coast which the government was worried about, because it was possible that the French could make a successful landing there, was Pevensey Levels. This area of wetland, the largest in East Sussex and situated between Eastbourne and Bexhill, is almost opposite Boulogne and was not protected by any batteries. It was therefore decided to build Martello towers there, with Colonel Twiss superintending the works.

The towers from Pevensey to Beachy Head were mainly built of superior London bricks from Adam and Robertson of Old Bond Street, while other towers in the county were built from cheaper bricks. No doubt profit for the individual builders was a factor. The cost of bricks at the time was between £2 and £3 per thousand, which sounds quite cheap until you consider the number of bricks that it took to build a single tower. A number of local brickmakers opened up new works to provide for this need, and there were a number of them between Eastbourne and Winchelsea, one standing east of Pevensey Castle.

In April 1805 William Pitt and Lord Castlereagh, the war minister, visited Lord Chatham, Pitt's elder brother, at Eastbourne. While they were there they went to look at the Martello towers that were under construction. Pitt must have been very interested, considering the role he played in the decision to build them.

The troops who manned the Martello towers were from various parts of the country, and their postings often changed. In 1805 the Derbyshire Militia was due to be based at the Martellos in the east of Sussex.

Many of the towers saw more action in the war against smuggling than they did in the war against France. The Coastal Blockade service operated in Sussex in the period between the end of the war and 1831, when the Coastguard finally took over their duties. It was in Kent and Sussex that much English smuggling took place, and it was where the smugglers seemed to be the most violent and well organised. In February 1822 it was reported in *The Times* that 'Sussex Fair Traders' were taking advantage of the dark nights by making attempts on all parts of the coast – but failed where they came across the Blockade men. On 11 February a mob of 300 smugglers went to Crow Link Gap near Eastbourne and grabbed two of the members of the Blockade posted there. Another guard saw what was happening, fired his gun and scared them off. Reading about gangs of hundreds of men being scared off by a few Blockade men makes you wonder just how violent these gangs really were. Just a few days later, on 15 February, a cargo was landed by smugglers at Seaford, at that time beyond the limits of the Blockade system. Some of the cargo was seized by the Preventive Waterguard, but the smugglers managed to get away with the rest. A few days later a gang attacked the men stationed at Tower 52.

In January 1828 a lugger landed a load between Bexhill and a public house called the Bo Peep. The cargo was carried off by a large gang of men using carts. The local Blockade men were too few in number to tackle them, so they called for reinforcements from the local towers. A group of Blockade men numbering around forty finally caught up with the smugglers at a village called Sidley Green. Many of the smugglers were armed, not only with their normal bats but also with guns, and in the ensuing battle two men from each side were killed, and several were wounded. The smugglers got away, and to try and catch them an officer of the Bow Street Runners was sent to the area. The newspaper report on the battle states that most of the gang were men from inland, labourers on low wages who were tempted to play a part by rich smugglers. They were probably less prone to using violence than the hardened smugglers who made a good living from the trade.

The Coastal Blockade service was severely depleted in August 1829, according to *The Times*, when many of the men stationed around Eastbourne were sent to the *Hyperion*, which was moored at Newhaven and about to be sent to the Mediterranean. It would appear that the Coastal Blockade's days were already numbered. Two years later the force was disbanded completely, and in 1835 newspaper advertisements were placed regarding the sale of military houses and stables at Eastbourne, and parcels of land of up to 1 acre at Bexhill, where Martello towers had previously stood. By 1852 most towers in Sussex were occupied by the Coastguard.

Surveys of coastal defences did not stop at the end of the war. In October and November 1845 the Duke of Wellington surveyed the East and South East Coasts, and sent his report to Sir George Murray, the Master-General of Ordnance.

In 1853 there was a report in the *Hampshire Telegraph and Sussex Chronicle* that the Martello towers in Sussex currently used by the Coastguard were being taken over by the Ordnance Department for the use of the Royal Artillery, and the Deputy Controller General of the Coastguard was trying to find alternative accommodation for his men. It seems that this either did not happen or did not last long, as a report in the local press in January 1855 states that the Royal Sussex Artillery Militia were going to be used for coastal duty at Eastbourne, and would occupy many of the empty Martello towers.

In 1867 advertisements appeared in the press for tenders for Army contracts to supply bread and meat to military establishments, including Towers 28 to 38, 39 to 49, 50 to 73 and Eastbourne Redoubt.

Around this time the Duke of Richmond, Lord Lieutenant of Sussex, stated that artillery volunteers should be used to man the guns in the towers only after they had been trained by an experienced artilleryman. There was a severe shortage of trained artillerymen, so this seemed like a good plan – and it became reality at a later date, when the invalids battalions of the Royal Artillery were formed. In the eighteenth century men enlisted in the Royal Artillery for life, which meant that the force included a number of men who were either too old or unfit for active service. However, they could be used to man batteries and train local men to fire large guns.

Of all the towers featured in this book, it seems that those in Sussex were most affected by the Second World War, being most altered to allow modern features.

Tower 28

This tower is situated at Rye Harbour by the River Rother and is known as the Enchantress Tower. I have read a number of explanations for this name. The one that has most currency is that it is down to the site of the tower, which is indeed enchanting. Another explanation connects it with a sloop named the HMS *Enchantress*, which was used by the Coastal Blockade men and based in Rye Harbour from 1819. It was quarters for a number of Blockade men, mainly landsmen with some naval training. Some were Irish labourers, who signed on for three years.

The tower was built on a knoll of shingle to the west of the harbour entrance under the direction of the civil engineer Sir John Rennie, engineer to the Admiralty as his father had been. Father and son were responsible for the construction of some of the bridges across the Thames and several dockyards.

In a report in 1873 the tower was described as in a favourable position to defend the harbour (it was armed with a 7-inch BL gun), although it was exposed to fire from the sea. This would have been difficult to remedy. The protection of Rye Harbour was not seen as a priority, and it was suggested that barges filled with shingle could be sunk in the entrance, shutting off the harbour in the event of an attack. Despite this plan, it was recommended that the tower be strengthened and improved. It was already moated, and its armaments were updated when it was given one of the Armstrong guns that were used to destroy some of the other Sussex towers in 1860. (Unused towers were sometimes used in gun trials.) There was also a suggestion that a battery of two or

Tower 28 is at Rye Harbour on a caravan site. It is surrounded by a wall, which does impede the view of the tower. There are also a number of Second World War defences around the area.

three guns could be erected near Camber Coastguard Station on the eastern side of the harbour.

There have been major changes in the coastline in this area, and the tower is now situated almost a mile from the sea. A number of Second World War defences were built close by, and some of these still exist. The tower, now on a caravan site but visible from the gate, is shut up and not in use.

Tower 29

Situated near the harbour mouth opposite Tower 28, Tower 29 was hardly used, as it became unsafe owing to encroachment by the sea soon after it was built, together with the removal of a large groyne to its east. A report on the effects of the sea on the tower was carried out by Lieutenant-Colonel C. G. Ellicombe of the Royal Engineers on 24 January 1820, and it was not favourable. By 1822 the brickwork was already cracking.

It is thought that Tower 29 was the tower sold for £200 that Cobbett mentioned in *Rural Rides*, but it was far from a bargain: it fell down just after it had been purchased. It was the first of the towers to vanish.

Tower 30

This is another inland tower, built on low ground to the west side of Rye on the Winchelsea Road. It was built to protect the sluices of the Royal Military Canal, where

Tower 30 is in the garden of a house which is set in a small gated estate on the main A259 road. (Ron Strutt)

the tidal water backs out from the canal, the River Brede and Pett Level. Tower 30 was one of only two with a wet moat; the other was at Clacton, Essex. In 1873 it was described as valuable in protecting the sluices, and therefore to be retained as a magazine: at this time it was unarmed. Part of the drawbridge still survives and nothing has been added to the roof.

Although converted into a dwelling after the Second World War, Tower 30 is currently empty. It is visible from the road but stands in a small private area that has entrance gates.

Tower 31

This was the first of a group of eight towers at Pett Level, and was also a semaphore station. It was washed away by coastal erosion at the end of the nineteenth century.

Tower 32

The second Pett Level tower was used as a Coastal Blockade hospital from 1827 – although hospital may be too grand a description, as it was essentially a standard tower manned by an assistant surgeon and the wives of some of the men. The tower was occupied by a Coastguard boatman in the nineteenth century. It was later washed away by coastal erosion.

Tower 33

This Pett Level tower was occupied by a Coastguard boatman in the nineteenth century, and according to most accounts was washed away by coastal erosion. However, a report in the *Hampshire Telegraph and Sussex Chronicle* in January 1889 states that it was destroyed in 1889 by Sir F. Abel and Captain Thompson of the Royal Artillery, using blasting gelatine. The account says that this was the first time this material was used to destroy a tower, and three 50-lb charges reduced the tower to rubble. If the tower had already been damaged by erosion, this discrepancy may be explained.

Tower 34

This tower, also on Pett Level, was the site of a battle between the Coastal Blockade and smugglers in 1829. By this time the Blockade was seriously short of men, many having been drafted on to ships. When a gang of smugglers numbering between 80 and 100 gathered near the tower there were not enough Blockade men available to attack them. When more Blockade men finally arrived there was a short conflict, in which one smuggler died and four Blockade men were wounded, but the smuggled goods were safely taken away by the gang. The tower was later occupied by a Coastguard boatman, but had been destroyed by coastal erosion by the end of the nineteenth century.

Tower 35

Another of the Pett Level towers, this was also occupied by the Coastal Blockade but very late in the organisation's existence – in 1830. The tower was subject to erosion, as were the others in the area, and was demolished as unsafe in the late nineteenth century. This was carried out in a explosives trial in which the tower was filled with 800 lbs of gun cotton (invented by a Mr Abel), then ignited. The event was reported in the *Hastings News* in April 1872 and in the *Graphic* on 11 May. The tower was blown up just before noon, and the experiment was successful: it was completely destroyed, being reduced to large pieces of masonry. The weather during this experiment was described as delightful, and large crowds gathered on higher ground 300 to 400 yards away to watch the destruction of this tower and also Tower 38, which was blown up a few hours later. The officers in charge of the experiment stayed at the Queen's Hotel.

Tower 36

This Pett Level tower was occupied by a Coastguard boatman in the nineteenth century, and was then partly washed away by erosion. The *Hastings News* reported that an important experiment with gun cotton took place at the tower, and it was described as the third tower to be rendered famous by Dr Gale's experiments. The tower, with walls 12 feet thick at the base, was safely demolished with 200 lbs of gun cotton in 5-inch discs, which was divided into three charges and fired at the same time by electricity. Not a single brick was blown more than 50 yards from the tower during the explosion.

Tower 37

The Coastal Blockade occupied this Pett Level tower, but again in 1830, late in the organisation's existence, as an additional station. Some of the towers were occasionally used as prisons to hold captured smugglers, and in 1830 some of these prisoners were held with the permission of local magistrates. It was rare for magistrates to support the Blockade against smugglers. The tower was partly washed away by coastal erosion and was eventually demolished in 1866 by the Royal Engineers.

Tower 38

This was the last tower on Pett Level, at the end of the Royal Military Canal at Cliff End. The tower was used by the Coast Blockade and was the scene of a vicious conflict between the Blockade men and smugglers in 1827. An alarm was given by a Blockade man when he was surrounded by smugglers and had to fight his way out. When men from the tower arrived a running fight took place, resulting in the deaths of three smugglers and the wounding of three men from Tower 38.

The tower was later occupied by a Coastguard boatman, but was partly washed away by coastal erosion and finally demolished in April 1872, in the same explosive experiment that demolished Tower 35. The material being tested was described as Stowmarket gun cotton, which had been stored at Upnor near Chatham. The experiments were conducted under the command of a Colonel Younghusband of the Royal Artillery. The explosive was used to destroy a number of buildings, starting with small wooden sheds and working up to brick-built magazines and finally the towers. The amount of gun cotton used to destroy the tower was 200 lbs, much less than had been used on Tower 35. In one of the previous experiments small discs of gun cotton weighing 7½ ounces had blown a hole in a brick wall 13 inches thick. The gun cotton used to destroy the tower was placed in three heaps on the basement floor. The explosion was due to take place at three o'clock but was instead carried out at 1.30 p.m., causing a number of interested spectators to miss it.

Tower 39

This tower was situated at St Leonard's and was occupied by the Coastal Blockade in 1830 as an additional station, like Tower 35 and Tower 37. The tower was visited by the Prince of Wales in 1864. By 1873 it had been badly damaged by coastal erosion and a bad storm, and after partial collapse three years later it was demolished. The *Hastings News* reported that the tower was damaged by heavy gales in the spring of 1876 and was eventually brought down in July by a group of workmen under a Mr E. Bull, the materials purchased by a Mr Briscoe. Mr Bull was complimented on the skilful manner in which he had conducted the mining operation on the massive walls, which in places were 9 feet thick. Mr Bull seems to have had more luck than other contractors, who usually had to call in the Army to complete the demolition of towers.

Tower 40

The tower was occupied by the Coastguard but then partly collapsed, undermined by the sea, and was eventually blown up by the Royal Engineers in 1873. They used two charges of gun cotton, the first consisted of 176 lbs and the second 126 lbs.

Tower 41

This tower was situated at Bulverhythe. From 1827 the tower (like Tower 32) was used as what was perhaps grandly called a Coastal Blockade hospital. No doubt it provided a much-needed service, as injury during attacks by smugglers appears to have been quite common. Any medical attention must have been appreciated.

The tower suffered damage from coastal erosion and was then demolished, the building materials being sold in 1842. There was a legal wrangle over their ownership, and they were then washed into the sea – thereby solving the ownership problem. Some of the material that was saved was reused to build St Mark's church, Little Common, Bexhill – as was the brick from Tower 42.

There is a rumour that this and Tower 42 were demolished to make way for the London, Brighton & South Coast Railway but this was built much further inland; the tower's position could not have been relevant.

Tower 42

This tower was also at Bulverhythe, and was occupied by the Coastal Blockade in 1830 as an additional blockade station. It was later used by the Coastguard.

The end of the Coastal Blockade service was not the end of battles with smugglers. In 1832, in a battle at Bexhill between smugglers and the Coastguard there were two fatalities among the Coastguard men. One of the men, William Meekes, was based at Tower 42. Both the men who died were shot. It is not clear if the Coastguard, a civil organisation, had the same problems as the Coastal Blockade men did when they hurt or killed smugglers.

The tower suffered damage from erosion in 1840 and was then demolished. As mentioned above, some of the material was used to build the church at Little Common.

Tower 43

This tower was built on the cliff tops at Bulverhythe Bay, and was lost to erosion by the early twentieth century. Although it seems that the low-level towers were the most vulnerable as they were nearer the sea, some of the towers built on higher cliffs (like this one) were in danger when the cliffs themselves collapsed.

Tower 44

Also built on the cliffs at Bulverhythe Bay, Tower 44 was used by the Coastal Blockade from 1818 to 1831. In 1821 a Blockade man named England was examining the nets of a local fisherman named John Swain – something that fishermen always complained about as they claimed it damaged the nets. After a scuffle between the men, Swain was shot dead. England was arrested, as witnesses said he had taken out his pistol and shot the fisherman. The Blockade man's version of events was very different; he said that Swain had thrown him off the boat, followed him ashore and knocked his cutlass from his hand. As Swain tried to take England's pistol from him it went off, accidentally shooting the fisherman. A hostile crowd gathered, and it was only when parties arrived from Tower 44, Tower 45 and other nearby blockade stations, as well as local cavalry, that the situation was brought under control.

England, as with other Blockade men who killed, was put on trial for murder – during which the locals swore he deliberately shot Swain, but Blockade witnesses denied this. The judge's summing up was biased in England's favour, as he saw through the local animosity, but despite this the jury still found the Blockade man guilty. England was sentenced to death but was given a free pardon.

Smuggling was at its height as men came home from the war and had no other way to make a living. On 3 January 1828 there was a large battle near here, later known as the Battle of Sidley Green, between smugglers and the Coastal Blockade men, including men from this tower. The smugglers were armed with lumps of wood, and fought the Blockade men, who had swords and muskets. There was a fatality on both sides, and the smugglers who were caught were transported.

The tower was lost to erosion in the early twentieth century, when it fell off the cliff.

Tower 45

This was situated near where the Sackville Hotel now is. It was the first of a long line of low-lying towers, and it was gone by the mid-nineteenth century, thanks to coastal erosion.

Tower 46

In 1830 this tower was twinned with Tower 44 to make a single blockade post. It was demolished in 1870, and the De La Warr Pavilion now stands nearby.

Tower 47

This tower was near Polgrove. It vanished in the mid-nineteenth century, shortly after appearing on maps dated 1844.

Tower 48

In 1830 Tower 48 was twinned with Tower 49 to make one blockade post. This seems to have been common procedure towards the end of the Blockade's life. Perhaps it was a way of saving on the number of officers after the organisation had lost men to the

Royal Navy. The tower was situated south of where Pages Avenue is today. There seems to be some confusion over the demise of this tower. *The Morning Post* of 3 November 1860 mentioned a planned artillery experiment at a Bexhill tower the following week. A report in the *Daily News* on 13 November 1860 mentions the experiment in relation to towers, not a single tower.

Tower 49

This tower was near Veness Gap. It was used for target practice by two 32-pounders and two 68-pounders on Cooden Down in November 1860. Unused towers were prime targets for experiments with new guns. As with Tower 48 there seems to be some confusion. Sutcliffe states that the fate of this tower was not known. Clements states that it was destroyed by artillery.

Tower 50

In 1824 Tower 50 was the site of a battle between smugglers and Blockade men. When a small group of Blockade men caught smugglers unloading a boat near the tower, one of them jumped into the boat, which then pulled away from the shore. The next morning his body was washed up on the beach. Murder was sometimes resorted to by smugglers in order to keep their identity secret.

Tower 50 featured in another fight in December 1825. A Blockade man named Mallowney chased and captured, after a fight, a smuggler named Wicks – who was taken back to the tower and held there until the end of January 1826, before being released without charge. This is just one example of a tower being used as a prison.

Again there does seem to be some confusion among other writers as to the fate of this tower. According to the *Hampshire Advertiser* of 24 November 1860, the tower was destroyed during experiments by the Royal Artillery with new guns. The experiments were watched by a huge crowd of spectators, including the Duke of Cambridge. According to the report the crowd had to be moved by the threat of guns being fired over their heads as they would not move away from the tower. The tower stood near the site of the Cooden Beach Hotel.

Tower 51

Although there were numerous cases of violent exchanges between smugglers and Blockade men, the smugglers sometimes used other methods to achieve their goals. In 1819 two men tried to bribe one of the Blockade men based in a tower at Bexhill. They offered him £100, an enormous amount at that time, to ignore what he saw, but he refused. Perhaps this indicates that some of the Blockade men had higher standards than is often suspected.

From 1827 this tower, which stood at Cooden, was used as a Blockade hospital. It had been lost to erosion by the end of the nineteenth century.

Tower 52

Also at Cooden, Tower 52 was actually subjected to an attack, though by smugglers rather than the French. At three o'clock on 23 February 1822 a large gang of smugglers arrived here and tried to seize the Coastal Blockade sentinel who was on duty, as there was a boat ready to land contraband nearby. It seems that the smugglers decided to put the Blockade men out of action before the landing, rather than fighting them during the event. When the sentinel was attacked he drew his pistol and shot one of the smugglers dead. The boat set sail and the alarm was raised. More Blockade men arrived, and captured one of the gang.

The tower was lost to erosion not long after the end of the nineteenth century.

Tower 53

This tower was also at Cooden, and was built together with Tower 54 to protect a Pevensey sluice. In 1830 a number of Blockade men were attacked near the tower by smugglers, leaving four of them seriously injured. The station commander, Lieutenant Goodridge, only arrived when the attack was over. There seems to have been some doubt over his stomach for a fight, and it was suspected that his late arrival was intentional. Goodridge was replaced by a Lieutenant Pennington. The tower had been lost to erosion by the end of the nineteenth century.

Tower 54

This tower, at Cooden, was also used by the Coastal Blockade. Those stationed in the towers had some advantages over their colleagues aboard ships. Provisions for the shore men were bought locally, and were much fresher than the food that men on the ships were given – which was often on board for months before it was eaten. On one occasion the provisions from Tower 54 were being stolen, and it turned out that the culprit was a deserter from Tower 55. Theft of goods from Blockade stations was not that rare; it was often rum that went missing.

The tower was sold in 1908 and demolished soon afterwards.

Tower 55

This tower, at Norman's Bay, supported the battery at Rockhouse Bank. It was originally one of the signal stations based on Martello towers and was used to send semaphore messages. Later adapted as a telegraph station in the early twentieth century, it was used as a machine gun post during the Second World War.

In 2004 it went up for sale, with planning permission to be used as a residence. A report in the *Sunday Times* stated that there was planning permission for conversion to a two-bedroom home with a kitchen, dining room, bathroom, study and living room. There was also permission for a glass extension on the roof. The estimated cost of conversion was £80,000, and the plans needed the agreement of English Heritage before

There is a big space between the last tower, Tower 30, and the next surviving one, which is Tower 55. It is known as Billy's Tower.

When I visited the tower in 2009 it was surrounded by scaffolding and a large plastic sheet while work was being carried out on it.

work could proceed. The disadvantages were obviously outweighed by the advantages: the guide price was between £130,000 and £150,000 but it sold for £285,000.

In 2008 the Second World War adaptations on the roof were demolished, along with the original chimney. Just as the Martellos meant little to the Victorians, who were only too eager to knock them down, Second World War remains appear to mean as little to us.

When I visited the tower in April 2009 it was surrounded by what looked like a large plastic bag, although there was a gap through which I could take a photograph. The tower appeared to be in good condition. I presume that the 'bag' is protecting the brickwork as alterations proceed.

Tower 55 is still quite remote. The houses that line the beach look more like holiday homes than permanent homes and the campsites and wonderful round chalets nearby, perhaps inspired by the tower, give the whole area of Normans Bay a holiday atmosphere. If you approach the tower via the road on the opposite side of the railway line, you have to cross a manually operated level crossing to reach the coast.

Tower 56

This tower was situated at Pevensey Bay and was occupied in the mid-nineteenth century. It was a victim of erosion some time after it was last mentioned, in 1873.

One of the towers in Pevensey Bay (unfortunately the report does not tell us which one) received a distinguished visitor shortly after its construction, when on 24 June 1805 the Duke of Cambridge reviewed the King's German Legion, based at Bexhill. The following day he rode to 'the Martello tower' that was being built in Pevensey Bay. Although the duke was full of praise for the King's German troops, it seems that not all of them were happy to be serving him in England. According to the *Chelmsford Chronicle* in November 1810, five men of the Legion stole a boat from the beach at Bexhill and were not seen again: it was believed that they were trying to reach the enemy shore. It is not known if they succeeded or if they were lost at sea.

Tower 57

Also situated at Pevensey Bay, Tower 57 was occupied by the Coastguard for much of the nineteenth century. It was a victim of coastal erosion in the early twentieth century.

When a smuggler named John Apps from Witling was fishing up tubs of spirits near a sluice at Pevensey, he was shot by a sailor from one of the Martello towers and died. The inquest found that his death was murder by persons unknown.

Tower 58

This Pevensey Bay tower was occupied for much of the nineteenth century, possibly by the Coastguard. It was demolished in the 1920s.

Tower 59

At Pevensey Bay, this tower was used by the Coastal Blockade. In 1830 the tower was twinned with Tower 62 to become a single blockade post. It was demolished in 1903 to make way for the building of a housing estate. The *Navy and Army Illustrated* of 4 July 1903 contains a photograph of a group of men with horses and carts demolishing the tower.

Tower 60

Situated at Pevensey Bay near the village, this tower was built on a stone plinth rather than straight onto the beach. The Coastguard used it in the early nineteenth century and a cottage was built by them nearby. It was owned by the War Office, and was used by the Cinque Ports Artillery Volunteers to practise firing large guns. It was re-armed with a more modern gun in 1873. It was then left to decline, and was almost derelict when the Royal Observer Corps took it over until the 1980s. It was partly restored with the addition of a new staircase, and once the Observer Corps stopped using the building it was sold for £22,000, renovated and made into a house.

This tower and the others remaining at Pevensey Bay give some idea of what the coast must have looked like when there was a continuous chain of towers. A ship in the bay could have been within range of the guns of fifteen towers at once. Unfortunately modern building means that the remaining towers are not as easy to see as in the past.

Tower 60 is now a well-kept residence standing among other houses.

This tower has been converted into a lovely-looking home with a nice garden. I imagine that anyone with an interest in history would be happy to live here.

Tower 61

This is one of the few towers that does not seem to have been used by the Coastal Blockade or by the Coastguard. It was built on a stone plinth. Left empty for much of the nineteenth century, Tower 61 was occupied by a farmer just after the First World War. It was used by the Canadian Army and the Home Guard during the Second World War as a gun emplacement, and had a battery and observation post built on it. These additions have been incorporated into the living accommodation, and they are still visible. The tower was close to a coastal battery, which was built in 1941 and manned by the Royal Artillery. It is now surrounded by a housing estate with a neat park around it, and the tower is in the central part of the estate. When I visited it had a temporary fence surrounding it for some reason.

Tower 62

This tower, also in Pevensey Bay, was used by the Coastal Blockade and then the Coastguard during the nineteenth century. It was known as the Grey Tower and is now on a caravan site of the same name. It was converted into a house before the Second World War, but became derelict after being requisitioned by the military. Offered for sale for £25,000 in 1973, the tower is now a home again. It is not possible to get

Tower 61 is a residence but when I visited in April 2009 it had a fence around it that seemed to be restricting access.

Tower 62 is known as the Grey Tower and the caravan site it stands on has the same name. At the beginning of the lane leading to the site is a small model tower.

Tower 62 seems in good repair and is a residence. It is surrounded by caravans.

close to the tower without going onto the caravan site, which had a barrier across its entrance when I visited. There is, though, an interesting small model tower at the top of the private road leading to the site.

Tower 63

Used by the Coastguard in the nineteenth century, Tower 63 became part of a shingle extraction operation that surrounded it during the 1930s. According to Sutcliffe the tower was destroyed by enemy action during the Second World War, but this cannot be verified from any other source. It appears it was demolished by the Royal Engineers, and the rubble was used to build an airfield at Friston.

Tower 64

Both the Coastal Blockade and the Coastguard used Tower 64 in the nineteenth century. It was sold by the War Office in 1910 and was occupied after the First World War. Re-armed and used during the Second World War, the tower still has modern machine-gun posts on it. Today it is known as Herds Tower, after a man who used it to store fishing nets in it. After the Second World War a number of old anti-tank blocks were left around the base of the tower.

Tower 64 is surrounded by large concrete blocks which were used as tank defences in the Second World War.

The Duke of Devonshire's family trust built a new marina nearby, and the Sovereign Harbour is now surrounded by a very upmarket housing estate: you have to go through this to find the tower. After passing these new luxury homes the tower looks quite desolate, standing alone on the beach and surrounded by the anti-tank concrete blocks. It is a pity that the tower cannot be used as part of the estate in some way. There is a clear view of Tower 66 across the harbour entrance from Tower 64.

Tower 65

This tower was sold by the War Office in 1910, together with Tower 64. It was occupied in the 1930s until the sea began to reach it, and it fell down just before the Second World War began. Some remains can still be seen at low tide.

Tower 66

Just east of Langney Point, Tower 66 was associated with the Crumbles Rifle Range and was close to Langney Redoubt, built at the end of the eighteenth century. The tower was used by the Coastguard from the nineteenth century until the 1990s, when it became unsafe as water began to leak in. Despite this leakage the tower still survives today, although it is derelict.

Above left: A view of Tower 66 taken from Tower 64. Tower 65 would have stood between them.

Above right: Tower 66 stands on the beach behind a new housing estate.

Tower 66 became the crest of Eastbourne Borough Football Club, which at the time of writing is in the Blue Square Premier league. The club was previously known as Langney FC.

This is another tower that has been surrounded by a new housing estate, and a high fence stops visitors approaching it. There must be access from the beach at some point, but I was unable to find it.

Tower 67

One of the group west of Langney Point, this tower was used by the Coastal Blockade. A record of those living in the tower survives, and indicates how difficult living conditions must have been. The midshipman in charge was named Mitchell, and he was supposedly in fear of a Mrs Oliver, who I take it was the wife of one of his men. Mrs Oliver had a violent temper, and was eventually expelled from the tower for this reason. Captain McCulloch himself commented on the case, saying that the wives of the men stationed at these bases were often troublesome enough to throw the whole party into confusion.

Later in the nineteenth century Tower 67 was occupied by the Coastguard, and then the Royal Artillery. It was still standing until the First World War, but began to collapse just after the war ended. The remains were demolished in 1922.

Tower 68

This tower stood 2 miles inland on St Anthony's Hill, and was built to protect the redoubt at Eastbourne rather than the coast. It was on the site of a battery, dating from the late eighteenth century, which had stood between the Langney Forts. The east fort had six guns and the west fort had eleven.

The tower was occupied for some time by a pensioner from the Sappers. The battery here was used in artillery firing experiments in November 1870, when the guns fired on one of the towers on the beach. Tower 68 was sold by the War Office in 1904 to Alderman J. T. Wenham, and demolished soon afterwards.

Part of the tower still remains, in the foundations of the house later built on the site.

Tower 69

This also belonged to the group of towers west of Langney Point that no longer exist. It was occupied by a member of the Royal Artillery in the mid-nineteenth century. The tower began to fall down in the late nineteenth century and may also have been used for artillery target practice, but I cannot confirm this.

Tower 70

In the mid-nineteenth century Tower 70 was occupied by a Royal Artillery pensioner. On 8 August 1860 the tower was used by a party of Royal Engineers, who set up a telegraph

Destruction of some of the towers was caused by artillery experiments. This old print from 1860 shows one of them destroyed by Sir William Armstrong's guns at a distance of 1,032 yards. The tower was one of those near Eastbourne.

station to report on the artillery experiment at Tower 71. They used the tower because of the very bad weather on the second day of the experiment and on safety grounds; their telegraph had previously run from a tent behind the battery to a small brick building by Tower 70, and there was a chance that this could be affected by flying debris.

The telegraph group was under the command of Captain Schaw and came from Chatham to take part in the experiment. At one point the telegraph wire was cut by a shell splinter, which showed the good sense of moving into Tower 70. The telegraph was reported to have been very useful: there was no need to use mounted orderlies to take messages, and during bad weather, when the bugles could not be heard or the flags seen from the battery, it was essential.

The tower began to fall down in the 1870s and was a ruin by the time further artillery experiments began in 1876. The ruins were used for target practice to see the results of shells striking on masonry.

Tower 71

This tower was used by the Coastal Blockade and was obviously not one of its better-run posts. The man in charge, Lieutenant Moss, was found to be drunk when the divisional commander visited just before Christmas in 1825. The Blockade men were given tots of rum daily, as were sailors at sea, and the rum store in the tower was found to be short by 3½ gallons. As the lieutenant had been at the tower for less than a fortnight, he must have been drinking a considerable amount for this much to disappear in such a short time. Following the incident Moss was sent home on half pay. His replacement did not do much better. Lieutenant Parker was later found to have 'lost' 7 gallons of rum. He was also sent home on half pay, and had to pay for the missing supplies.

The tower was later taken over by the Coastguard, and was used as a target by the Royal Artillery when they were testing new guns in August 1860. These guns were designed by Sir W. G. Armstrong, who was present at the experiment, and were positioned near Tower 68 at Langney. The Duke of Cambridge and a large staff of artillery and other officers were also in attendance. Each of three guns fired seven or eight shots and the spectators were, according to the *Hastings News*, allowed to approach and see the damage caused by each shot. After about two hours a hole was finally made in the tower wall.

Allowing the public to approach after each shot seems like quite a strange decision. A more detailed report of the breaching experiment against Tower 71 was made for the Ordnance Select Committee by Lieutenant-Colonel W. O. Lennox, Royal Engineers, and Captain Bolton, Royal Artillery. Opening with some information about the tower itself, it stated that it was built in 1804 at a cost of £3,000, held twenty men and eighty barrels or seventy cases of powder, and that heavy Armstrong guns were used to demolish it. At the time of the experiment the tower was described as perfectly sound, with walls 7 feet 6 inches thick on the seaward side of the building. The sea reached the base of the tower at high tide, there was a watermark 9 feet from the ground on the tower and there was half a mile of shingle behind it. It seems that the decision was made to use the tower as it would have eventually fallen down anyway, because of the sea's encroachment.

The battery was beyond the turnpike road from Eastbourne to Pevensey, at Hoisey Farm, 1,032 yards from the tower. It consisted of an 82-pounder with a 6-inch calibre, a 7-inch howitzer firing 100-lb shells, and a 40-pounder which was 4.75 calibre. The experiment began on 7 August, when solid shot was fired from the 82- and the 40-pounder and shells from the howitzer. The first shot from the 40-pounder sunk 4 feet into the tower wall: the depth was measured by pushing iron rods into the holes. Each shot was logged and photographs were taken of the damage. The first ball from the 82-pounder sank 3 feet 2 inches into the wall. The shell from the howitzer hit the shingle in front of the tower and ricocheted over it. The tower had begun to crack slightly by the sixth shot, and the seventh went right through the wall. There was a mixture of solid shot and shells used, and by the twenty-seventh shot there were some holes in the wall of the tower. The experiment continued the following day but torrential rain and strong winds made the process difficult. It also led to the range-finding party taking shelter in Tower 70, along with the telegraph group.

It took seventy-two shots before the central pillar of the tower was destroyed. By the end of the second day most of the front of the tower had been destroyed but the

Other towers were destroyed by experiments with new forms of gunpowder and gun cotton. The print shows another tower near Eastbourne being blown up using Gale's Protected Gunpowder.

back was hardly damaged. The spectators were kept at a distance of 500 yards, and there is no mention of them being allowed to come closer and examine the damage. Perhaps the local newspaper confused the spectators with military officers who were part of the experiment, and no doubt wanted to see the damage close up after each shot.

After the experiment came to an end, several live shells were left inside the ruins of the tower. A notice was posted by the chief constable, Colonel Mackay, warning of the unexploded shells and the dangerous conditions of the tower remains. Despite this, in October a builder named Jabez Reynolds employed two men to clear the rubbish in the tower – and among this rubbish there were two shells, which were placed on the beach. Corporal Harry, Private Anderson and Private Brown of the 91st Foot went to look at them. Anderson said there was powder in one of the shells and Brown said he would get it out – which he did by putting paper in a hole and lighting it. The other two soldiers seemed to have more sense and ran away. Brown was seriously injured when the shell blew up, and died a few hours later. F. W. Moore, in charge of the Military Hospital at Eastbourne, arrived at the scene shortly afterwards, and asked if the men had orders to deal with the shells. He was told that Lieutenant-Colonel Lennox of the Royal Engineers had told them to report any shells that were found to Sergeant Robinson. A verdict of accidental death was given at the inquest held at the Marine Tavern.

Tower 72

Also west of Langney Point, this tower was used as a Coastal Blockade station. From 1827 it was also a Blockade hospital, and later was used by the Coastguard. It was sold by the War Office in 1888 to Carew Davies-Gilbert, when it was being used by local fishermen. They were told by the tower's new owner not to spend any money on the land surrounding it as he had plans for it. The tower no longer exists.

Eastbourne Redoubt

The construction of this redoubt began in 1805 on 17 acres of land that were rented from the Lord of the Manor of Eastbourne for £48 a year. The building contractor was William Hobson, who had built the Old Bailey in London. He employed a number of local builders to help with the project. It was completed in 1808 as part of the anti-invasion defences that included the Martello towers. A garrison of around 200 men was based here, in twenty-four barrack rooms. It is interesting that the oven in the kitchen was said to be able to cook for 279 men, when the redoubt was actually capable of holding 350. Water came from four large internal tanks, which were topped up with rainwater. The men posted here slept in hammocks at first, but these were later replaced with beds. Lighting was by candle, although there was one lamppost in the centre of the parade ground. Tents were often pitched around this as accommodation for visiting troops. There were no married quarters; they were very rare for soldiers at this time. Later married quarters were built in Warrior Square, where many of the officers based here lived.

Defences included a dry moat and a drawbridge. There were supposed to be eleven guns but only ten were ever mounted. These were 24-pounders, but they were replaced with larger guns after the war. The gunpowder was kept in the magazine, but often had to be stirred to stop condensation damaging it. The guns were fired in anger during the Napoleonic Wars, a rare occurrence for these defences. In 1812 they fired on a French ship that had strayed too close to the coast – but they missed.

The men based at the redoubt and the local Martello towers added markedly to the prosperity of Eastbourne, which when they were built was quite a small town. By 1830, however, the number of men stationed at the redoubt had dwindled to seven gunners and a gatekeeper – and there was space for their families to move in. At this time it was very rare for families to live with serving soldiers. In 1834 the redoubt was also occupied by six boatmen of the Coastguard, and in 1841 a number of men were still living here with their families. Shortly after this the Duke of Wellington visited the redoubt, an event which was reported in the local press. He was accompanied by Lieutenant Conjuit of the Royal Navy, who was in command of the local Coastguard. The duke's opinion of the towers seemed to have risen after his visit.

The redoubt was also used as barracks for troops using the local Crumbles Rifle Range and a number of different regiments were stationed there at various times. In 1848 Sergeant Charles Bruce was in charge, and also responsible for thirteen of the local towers. This seems a huge responsibility for someone of his rank, especially as he was in his seventies.

The entrance to Eastbourne Redoubt, which is now a military museum.

The interior of the redoubt at Eastbourne. The design of the three redoubts were very similar.

The guns were replaced in the 1860s with larger weapons, and the redoubt was used during artillery experiments in November 1876. Live and dummy shells were fired at targets from guns in the redoubt and from the battery at St Anthony's Tower. This was watched by an attaché from the Italian embassy and General Sir J. Lintorn Simmons, the Inspector General of Fortifications. All did not go to plan: someone had cut the telegraph wires, so results of the firing could not be relayed from the targets to the guns.

There was some public concern locally at the amount of gunpowder stored in the magazine in the 1870s. If there had been an accident and the powder had exploded, much of Eastbourne could have been destroyed along with the redoubt.

The redoubt began to be used by others in the twentieth century. Groups such as the Church Lads' Brigade held their annual camps there. At the time of the First World War the Church Lads were much more military in nature than the Boys' Brigade. When the war began the redoubt was used by various groups, including naval reservists and the military police – who had cells in the building. It was also used as an observation post and a military hospital.

The redoubt was purchased by the local council for £150 after the First World War, which seems a bargain when the price asked in 1888 was £6,000. Between the wars it was opened to the public – but it was soon back in military hands, being requisitioned by the War Department in the Second World War, when it was used as military stores and an anti-aircraft battery. Plans to use the building as an air raid shelter were not followed through. It was occupied by Canadian troops before D-Day.

After the war the redoubt housed an aquarium and a model village, and in the 1970s a small museum was opened. Today it is a museum for the Royal Sussex Regiment and the Queen's Royal Irish Hussars. A Centurion tank of Korean War vintage is parked outside.

Tower 73

The Wish Tower is named after a marsh close by, where Shomer Dyke enters the sea. The garrison of the tower consisted of twenty-four men and an officer, with the usual single cannon mounted on the roof. It was manned from 1808 until 1812 by the East Sussex Volunteer Corps, then by the Coastal Blockade and the Coastguard. A Blockade man died by the tower in April 1824 when he fell off the cliff in a thick fog. In 1833 there was a battle between the smugglers and the Coastguard: one coastguard officer was killed (the last to die in Eastbourne in violence associated with smuggling) and three were badly wounded.

After being occupied by the Royal Artillery, Tower 73 became the responsibility of the local corporation in about 1874. It was empty until 1886, when it was leased to the Hollobon family as a museum and a dwelling; they remained here until the 1930s. During the Second World War it was used as an observation post and magazine. Guns were positioned in front of the tower, although they were of First World War vintage and at one point were manned by the Home Guard. There were plans to demolish the tower after the war but it was saved – and later became a museum again. Today it is empty.

Right: Tower 73, the Wish Tower at Eastbourne.

Below: An old print from 1860 of the Wish Tower and Eastbourne.

Tower 74

It has been said on several occasions that Seaford Tower was the last of the Sussex towers to be built, in 1810. This cannot be true, as the tower was visited in May 1808 by Brigadier-General William Twiss. There is something different about the Seaford tower, however, as it is on its own with no other towers to support it: there is a huge distance between it and the nearest, Tower 73. This is also true of the tower at the other end of the line, in Aldeburgh, Suffolk.

Building was begun in either 1805 or 1806: the lease on the land at Seaford, £2 per acre per year, began in the summer of 1806. The builder was a Mr Seed and the surveyors were W. Turner and P. Lee, all local men. Tower 74 (which is one of those with a moat) was the most expensive of them all, costing £18,000. This seems an enormous amount compared with the other Sussex towers. There was a plan to build more towers as far along the coast as Littlehampton, but this never happened.

Perhaps one reason for the tower being alone was that it was supported by the Blatchington and Seaford batteries. These had been built in 1760. Seaford Battery was 700 feet west of the tower site. It had five guns, a magazine and accommodation for the troops who manned it. West Blatchington Battery was built to the east of the tower site in 1794. Barracks were added later, mainly occupied by militia. In 1795 a mutiny of the Oxfordshire Militia took place here, and was put down by regular troops. By 1870 the battery held six guns, and had become known as a fort rather than a battery.

Although the Coastal Blockade stations were mainly taken over by the Coastguard when the service was abolished in 1831, it was only in 1824 that the Blockade men had first taken over the tower at Seaford from the Coastguard. It was not long before the tower's residents had a tragedy to deal with. In 1826 Lieutenant Aitkin, who was based at the tower, fell overboard from a galley and was drowned.

In 1953 the need for Seaford Tower was doubted by Aubrey de Sélincourt in his book *The Channel Shore*. He thought that Seaford was a highly unlikely place for an enemy landing to occur, as even in moderate weather the sea breaks heavily on Seaford beach. Perhaps he was unaware that 1,500 Frenchmen landed in Seaford in 1545, to be driven off by the townspeople. If the French had ever managed to land successfully at Seaford, the town of Lewes would have been put at risk – which could have given the enemy a route into London.

In 1828 the tower was occupied by the crew of HMS *Hyperion*, a customs cutter. It was also used as a temporary lock-up for captured smugglers. As smuggling declined so no further use was found for the building, and the construction of Newhaven Fort nearby in the late nineteenth century meant that there was no need to use the tower for defence, as the fort could protect the whole bay.

In 1880 the tower was purchased by a descendant of the builder, John Lee, and he turned it into a museum. There were plans for other uses, such as a library, but these did not happen. While the gun was being removed from the roof two years later, it fell and smashed the drawbridge.

The tower sold again just before the First World War, and was bought by Tom Funnell. It was used as a café, amusement arcade and roller-skating rink, and living accommodation was added to the roof. During the Second World War the tower was requisitioned, and Mr Funnell sold it afterwards – as its use as an amusement arcade was no longer seen as in keeping with the image of the area. It was purchased by the local council in 1948.

Despite being in danger of erosion from the sea, Tower 74 has survived. Since 1979 it has been Seaford Local History Museum, and part of the moat is used as a café. The first thing you notice as you approach the tower, apart from the fact that it still has a gun on top (it was replaced when the tower was renovated), is that it looks much smaller than other towers. Once you get close to it you can see why: on the seaward side the ground has been built up, so that it reaches some way up the tower.

Tower 74 at Seaford. The final East Coast tower, miles from the previous tower at Eastbourne.

5

ESSEX

As with the South Coast, there seem to have been constant surveys of the East Coast from the mid-1790s until the Martello towers were finally built. Although the obvious place for a French invasion would have seemed to be along the South Coast, which was closer to France, in the 1790s there was also a danger of invasion from Holland. A French Army numbering around 80,000 was based at Texel, and these men could have been carried to the East Coast by the Dutch fleet. Invasion from Holland was not unheard of, as in the seventeenth century the Dutch had sailed up the Thames and attacked Chatham, and also landed a force to attack Landguard Fort in Harwich Harbour.

The forces protecting the area were largely made up of militia regiments, whose usefulness in battle was not something that many relied upon. The object of many militia commanders seemed to be to dress their men in the fanciest uniforms they could afford. For example, the Revd Mr Dudley paid £260 for clothes for men in the Rochford and Chelmsford sub-divisions. It took two coaches to deliver the clothes, which included more than 100 green feathers. The officers of the volunteer units in Essex seemed to spend as much time attending military balls and taking part in amateur dramatics as they did in training to fight.

In April 1795 Captain Lewis Hay of the Royal Engineers reported on the likely landing places of an enemy force between Harwich and the mouth of the Crouch River. The building of several batteries was recommended at strategic points around the coast, but they don't seem to have been built straight away. There was a great outcry from the local people, who wanted Martello towers to be built in coastal areas: they were terrified of a French invasion. There were already a number of signal towers in Essex, at Great Clacton, Little Holland, Beacon Hill at Harwich and St Osyth. The naval lieutenant in charge of each of these was paid 7s 6d a day and had a midshipman and two seamen under his command; they lived in a house attached to the tower.

Captain Hay later returned to the East Coast with Brigadier-General Sir John Moore in 1797, by which time some of the batteries had been built – although many still did not have any guns. They agreed that that the 8 miles between Walton Gap and Clacton Wick were the most likely spots for an enemy attack. A landing at this point would put enemy forces only 12 miles from Colchester, which had a direct road to London. In 1798 a military report about the defence of the Eastern District, which included Lincolnshire, Norfolk, Suffolk and Essex, also found that the area around Clacton was the most likely spot for an enemy landing. It also pointed out other vulnerable areas, such as the Wallet, the Colne and the Maldon river estuaries. Suggestions given for defending these places were mainly naval ones, including gunboats at strategic points. The Sea Fencibles later patrolled some of the vulnerable areas on armed barges. The report also stated that there was no need to further protect Harwich Harbour, as ships entering the harbour had to pass under the guns of Landguard Fort on the Suffolk side of the harbour to get in. However, some protection was needed for the town.

A scorched earth policy towards invasion was still seen as feasible. The responsibilities for this policy were sorted out locally, as is illustrated by a meeting of the inhabitants of Fingringhoe in April 1798. The aim was to preserve property and draw away all cattle from the coast. Mr T. J. Page was given the responsibility of destroying mills and ovens and to mark cattle, assisted by L. Stone and John Archer. Edward Wade was appointed as the captain of fifteen men who would fell trees across roads. Tom Jaggard was captain of another twenty-five men. Steward King and P. Stone were conductors of wagons and carts, and John Cooper was inspector of wagons.

In June 1801 General Balfour, the Chief Commandant of the Eastern District, which included the Essex coast, completed a survey of the shore of the Blackwater River from Maldon to Bradwell. He gave directions to mount heavy ordnance at certain points, including the beach on Ramsey Island.

When the invasion scare of 1803 occurred there was a rush to sign up new volunteers, and they were quickly organised into groups. Although they may have only been armed with pitchforks, they knew the land and the network of dykes (and the paths through them) that protected the coast. Fighting in those days was a hand-to-hand business, and a pitchfork could do a lot of damage.

There were also more formal defences. In October 1803 Lieutenant Jones of the Royal Engineers, together with twenty-five men of the East Norfolk Militia, began to erect a battery on Hornet Heath near Wivenhoe, which was to hold two cannon to protect Wivenhoe ferry. Ten days after they began the ferry here was used to carry stores for the battery, consisting of shot, round and grape, gunpowder and four cannon – two of which were for the Hornet Heath battery and the others for one on the Strood.

A report on Essex's defences against invasion was carried out by the Royal Engineers in 1805. This recommended that thirty-two towers be built in the county, together with a circular battery at Harwich, rather than forts. By this time towers were already being planned for the South Coast. It was suggested that towers should be positioned on the River Crouch near St Peter's Chapel, on Mersea Island and at Harwich. However, as most of the previous reports had agreed that the coast from Walton-on-the-Naze to Clacton was most at risk of invasion, the towers were built along this part of the coast. Although in the report by the Royal Engineers the suggested towers had been numbered, they were known by letter rather than by number when they were built.

Square plots of land for the towers were purchased from local landowners. The total area came to 71½ acres for the eleven towers. Negotiations for the purchase of land began in 1808 under the direction of Colonel George Whitmore, commander of the Eastern district. Tower plans had already been prepared by Colonel Twiss and Captain Ford. Despite the grand plans of the initial report, land for only eleven towers was purchased. As an example, agreements relating to land for the towers at Clacton were made between George Samuel Wegg and King George III in 1810 at the price of £130 10s, and construction began the following year. While the agreement was being drawn up between the king and landholders, George was very ill. The king's health was one of the major subjects in the *Chelmsford Chronicle* in November 1810.

Building began in 1810, and many of the towers were not completed until a time when some believed that the danger of invasion had already passed. Local builders were used under the direction of an engineer. An advertisement was placed in the *Ipswich Journal* in 1808 by the Royal Engineers Office at Colchester, which stated that there was plumbing work to be done on the towers being erected on the coast, and called for tenders for the supply of solder. Bricks to build the towers came from various places throughout the South East, and one area that prospered thanks to this was Grays. The brick earth there had led to brick production as early as the beginning of the eighteenth century, and the sudden increase in demand may even have been the reason that some businessmen joined the trade. For example, Thomas Seabrooke owned a brewery in Grays from the beginning of the century – then bought nearby land and began brickmaking in about 1811, when the Essex towers were under construction.

The East Coast towers were slightly larger than those built on the South Coast and were slightly different in design. They had two staircases instead of one and were built to hold three guns instead of one, usually a 24-pounder and two smaller howitzers. The gun station on the roof had a quatrefoil layout, with the largest gun in the section facing the sea and the other guns either side. The towers had space for a garrison of fifty men, but because it was believed that the areas where the towers were built were unhealthy these garrisons were based at Weeley Barracks – built in 1803 to hold 4,000 men. The garrisons could reach any of the towers from Weeley within an hour. This decision to base the garrisons in one place did not find favour with everyone. The Earl of Chatham, Pitt's brother, maintained that the object should be to have the towers manned at all times, so that the garrisons, by 'constant habit', should be as confident in their tower as the smuggler in his boat. It was an interesting comparison considering the use many of the towers were put to after the Napoleonic Wars.

The whole of the Essex coast was dominated by troops during the conflict, an influence that was not just seen in the architecture of the towers. In Great Clacton, for example, the room on the upper floor of the Queen's Head Inn had a large bow window added and was used as a ballroom by officers based in the area.

After the Napoleonic Wars some of the Essex towers, as with those on the South Coast, were used by the Coastguard. Smuggling in Essex never reached the same scale or violence of that in Kent and Sussex, so the Coastal Blockade never operated in the county.

The towers were re-armed in 1830, a few years after the Napoleonic Wars ended, because of further threats from the unstable situation in Europe. In 1839 the new danger from France and her modern steamships led to calls to repair the towers in Essex, and even to build more. One was suggested for West Mersea, with three guns and to be used as a control point for electric mines.

Tower A is the first Essex tower. It is at Point Clear on a caravan site and is now an aviation museum.

The remoteness of the Essex coast can be seen by the census for 1861, which stated that Frinton-on-Sea had only twenty-nine inhabitants. There were so few people that a burial in the churchyard was a rare event. When the railway line was laid in 1865 from Colchester to Walton-on-the-Naze, Clacton was described as consisting of a couple of Martello towers, a few cottages, several farms and a few cart tracks.

In December 1870 the Tendring Board of Guardians was discussing precautions regarding cholera. They declined to make any provision for the sufferers, and a Colonel Montague informed the town clerk that the government had declined permission to use a Martello tower to house cholera patients. The alternative was a boat moored at Brightlingsea. Although some of the Sussex towers had been Coastal Blockade hospitals I have not heard of any being used as hospitals or quarantine stations for general diseases among the public.

In September 1919, 163 acres of land in Clacton, with a shore front of a mile and including two Martello towers, was put up for sale – according to *The Times*. The towers were described as generally lacking in light and air, but the article said that some adventurous types had attempted to live in them.

In 1930 the county's towers were described in the *Essex Review* as being for defence in theory only, as they were as much use against modern armaments as a sentry box. This did not stop many of the towers being used again in the Second World War.

Tower A

Tower A was built at St Osyth near the ferry to Brightlingsea, to protect the River Colne. The land was purchased from St Osyth's Priory. It was reported in *The Times* that in February 1811 the tower inclined because the ground had given way. The ground on the other side of the building was dug out, so that the tower would tip back in the other direction. The fact that this movement did not damage the tower was proof of how strong and resilient these buildings were.

The article by Commander Mead stated that the inhabitants of the tower had told him the basement of the tower had once been used to hold French prisoners of war during the Napoleonic Wars. Although I have not read this anywhere else it is quite possible, as numerous places were used to imprison a large number of French prisoners. A number of local buildings were used to house French officers on parole.

As with the towers in other areas, those in Essex did not see any conflict. At the end of the war it was decided to place pensioners from either the Artillery or the Sappers in the towers with their families, and they were paid a shilling a day on top of their pensions in return for, among other duties, keeping the towers aired, to prevent dampness. Smoking inside the building was not allowed. John Brewerton was the inhabitant of Tower A.

The tower was later taken over by the Coastguard. In 1848 *White's Gazetteer* mentioned three towers and a fort in St Osyth, all occupied by the organisation. Tower A continued to be used by them until the end of the nineteenth century.

The roof of Tower A, which was adapted for use in the Second World War. Windows have been cut into the wall, which gives a view across to Mersea Island.

The tower was used again during the First and Second World Wars, when new guns were added to the roof and an observation window was added inside to give views over the river estuaries of the Colne and the Blackwater. It was also possible to observe Brightlingsea, Mersea Island and Bradwell.

Since 1986 the tower has been occupied by the East Essex Aviation Society and Museum. There is a large entrance at ground level. The exhibits contain several aircraft that crashed locally during the Second World War, as well as large collections of weapons and medals. The tower is surrounded by a large caravan site.

Tower B

Tower B was built at Beacon Hill, St Osyth. Like its neighbour, Tower A, it has a view over the river as far as Mersea Island. The land that it was built on was farmed by John Tiles. Corporal Alex Watson inhabited the tower after the Napoleonic Wars. It was also used as a residence from just before the First World War, being occupied by a family named Cole. William Cole was one of the founders of the Essex Field Club. The tower was demolished in 1967 to make way for new houses – the last Essex tower to be demolished.

Tower C

Tower C was built on St Osyth beach at Bush Wall Point. It was occupied by Gunner Ruff after the Napoleonic Wars, and was used as a home and a café after being sold in 1908. Before the First World War a guard house and a magazine were built here, but they were eventually lost to the sea. The tower was put up for sale by the War Office in 1906, used by troops during the First World War, then in July 1918, before the war ended, put up for sale again. The sale included 3½ acres of land surrounding the tower. Tower C was again occupied by the Army during the Second World War.

In 2002 the local council commissioned a feasibility study to discuss the costs involved in restoring the tower, now surrounded by caravan sites, and the uses that it could be put to. There were suggestions of a home for the regimental organisation of the 95th Rifles, a regiment made famous by the Sharpe novels of Bernard Cornwell (himself from Essex) and their television spin-off. Another suggestion was for a permanent exhibition of the history of the village of St Osyth, including the 1953 floods. The tower has now been renovated and since 2005 it has been an arts centre. It is used by the local community for a number of leisure activities. It has its own website, and in an effort to get local people involved a friends group has been formed to give tours of the tower and talks.

Tower D

When Tower D was built at Eastness on Jaywick Farm the land was owned by George Wegg. Orders had been issued to secure marshland for Martello towers in 1808. A small stream flowing through the site was diverted to make a moat – making it one of only two towers to have a wet moat.

Tower C is at St Oysth and is now an arts centre that has been updated in the last few years.

Tower D now stands by Clacton golf course and is unused. This image shows how remote the tower still is.

A closer view of Tower D with Clacton in the distance.

According to Kenneth Walker, Tower D and Tower E were connected by a tunnel, which collapsed as a result of heavy seas in 1918.

The tower was occupied by a pensioner from the Sappers or the Royal Artillery after the Napoleonic Wars, and in 1817 the guardian was Gunner James Smith.

By 1826 there was concern at the encroachment of the sea towards the tower and the nearby battery. However, the sea walls protected the tower and the battery, which was in ruins by the time of the Second World War. Erosion of the beach eventually led to Eastness being removed from maps.

The tower was sold in 1904 and the land around it became a golf course a few years afterwards. During the First World War the tower was occupied by the Essex Cyclist Battalion. One of them sent a postcard that showed the men on top of the tower; on it he had written, 'Our little grey home in the west.' This tower and the next, Tower E, were alleged to be connected by a tunnel, which collapsed in 1918. I have come across a few mentions of towers with connecting tunnels (see also Tower J), but have found no proof of this.

The tower is now shut up and unused, and suffering from water damage. In 2008 the tower was placed on English Heritage's At Risk register.

Tower E

There was already a piquet house and battery close to the site where Tower E was built. The land had been rented from a man named John Smith in 1803 and a battery was erected in 1805. This was later used as an outer defence for the tower, which was built at Clacton Wash.

Although the tower was remote when it was built, by the Victorian period Clacton had begun to reach the area around it, west of the town. In the opposite direction the Napoleonic army camp that had once been occupied by Hessian troops was also covered in villas.

At the end of the nineteenth century a jetty was built by the tower, to be used by barges that brought building materials for new houses in the area. The barge owners found it easier to continue to run their craft up on the beach, and the construction became an amusement centre – like Clacton's pier.

The tower was occupied by a Peter McGee after the Napoleonic Wars, then sold in 1904. It was part of the West Clacton Estate and was used as a playground by children. The granddaughter of the estates manager remembered playing on the roof and in one of the dark rooms.

The jetty was of some use between the wars, when it was owned by Finch and Almond and converted into a small pleasure pier with amusements and cafés. Concerts were given there. When the Second World War began the jetty was blown up in case the Germans used it to invade. No doubt an invasion force would have found landing on the beach more convenient, just as the old barge masters had.

In 1936 the tower was sold to Butlins, together with the land around it, for a holiday camp. Shortly after this was built the Second World War began, so it was surrounded with barbed wire and became an internment camp for enemy aliens instead – although in the opinion of many it was still a holiday camp for those inside. Not only were all the Butlins camps taken over, but Billy Butlin actually began to build camps for the government – as he could do it cheaper than they could.

The Clacton camp was not used as an internment camp for long, and became a camp for the Pioneer Corps. In a flashback to the old days of unhealthy Essex coastlines, several members of the Corps based there died of pneumonia. Later it was an anti-aircraft base. The camp has now been replaced by a housing estate, and the tower stands unused in the car park.

In 2008 the tower was placed on the English Heritage At Risk register, because of water damage. The interior of the tower is in serious decline, and the floor is in danger of collapsing.

Tower F

There was already a signal station near the site of this tower, on Clacton Cliffs. This was higher than the previous towers, which were built on the seashore. The station stood on a hill that overlooked the beach, a natural choice for a signal station.

The choice of Clacton as a possible landing site for the French had a basis in fact: in 1797 a French privateer was driven ashore there, and the crew of around twenty men was captured by excise men and local farmers. Another reason for the choice of this site for a Martello tower was that there was a road nearby, which could have been used by a landing force to travel inland.

Tower E seen from Tower D. Clacton Pier is to the right.

A closer view of Tower E, which used to stand inside Butlins holiday camp but is now unused in a car park.

The building of the tower was not without controversy, however. When the builders began to use shingle from the beach local people complained – as the beach was a natural defence against an encroaching sea. Perhaps the use of shingle from beaches to build them explains why so many of the towers foundered so quickly.

In the article by Commander Mead it stated that the inhabitants of the tower had told him that the basement of this tower had also once been used to hold French prisoners of war during the Napoleonic War. Although I have not found this mentioned anywhere else it is quite possible. There were numerous places used to hold the large number of French prisoners in the country at the time. So any local strong buildings could have been used to hold French prisoners.

The tower was occupied by Sergeant-Major Baker after the Napoleonic Wars, and then by a Mr W. Hook, a member of the Tendring Board of Guardians. The tower became a Coastguard station in 1888, and still has an addition from this time (1888) on the roof; it is now unused. Cottages were built nearby for the Coastguard men and the tower was used as a lookout station. In the late nineteenth century the tower was the only building in the area, and its grounds were popular for parties by local people.

Before the First World War the Palace Theatre was built just behind the tower at a cost of £50,000. This had extensive grounds, with large attractions such as a Japanese pagoda. It later became a cinema.

Tower F was occupied by the Essex Regiment during the First World War. Some old guns from the nearby battery had been found and mounted nearby as ornaments,

Tower F is the nearest tower to the centre of Clacton and has been put to a variety of uses over the years.

but these were quickly hidden during the war – as Clacton could have been seen as an armed town, and attacked, if it had guns on display. This happened in other coastal towns that had antique weapons on show.

The tower was put to an unusual use in the 1920s. When new long-range guns were being tested at the Isle of Grain on the Kent side of the Thames, the tower was used to monitor the tests. The shells from these guns could travel 38 miles, which could take them off the coast at Clacton.

Later the tower became a museum, and during the Second World War it was again occupied by the Coastguard. When the war ended it became the headquarters of the local Sea Cadets and was known as the training ship *Clacton*.

The tower stands at Marine Parade close to the pier. This is unusual in that the other Essex towers are in more remote positions. It has been used for a number of leisure purposes recently because of this. It was a children's zoo in the 1970s, then the site of a model village.

The zoo in the tower came to an untimely end. In 1987 it was reported in *The Times* that an RSPCA inspector had found forty-three dead animals and birds after a complaint by a neighbour. This led to the zoo's owner being fined £600.

Although the tower may have protected Clacton from invasion, on occasions it let the town down. A weather station was fitted on the tower during the First World War and a computerised update was added in 1995. During a heatwave in the summer of 2001, however, the temperature shown at the tower was lower than the council's tourism manager would have liked – so the thermometer was moved to the town hall, where it is less affected by sea breezes and shows a higher temperature.

An older view of Tower F, without the later Coastguard construction on the roof.

In 2009 the tower was opened as a restaurant, still with its drawbridge and first-floor entrance. However, the *Clacton Gazette* of 5 March 2009 reported that a new use was being considered. The tower was for sale for £99,950, which seems very cheap in comparison with other towers sold recently, as illness was forcing the owners to sell up. The possible new owners were a couple, Dhirajlal and Sushila Karia, who had been running a Hindu temple from their Clacton home for thirty years and were interested in turning the tower into a temple and community centre. This idea was short lived, as a petition was raised locally against it and the Karias, deciding that they did not wish to upset any local people, cancelled the project. This led to a spate of letters to the local press, and allegations of racism. It was probably the greatest level of public interest that any of the Martello towers had inspired for some years. At the time of writing the restaurant remains closed.

Tower G

This was one of three towers that guarded Holland Marshes, and it was on a site that became known as Tower Hill. The government purchased 4 acres of land at Horsemarsh, at Great Holland Hall near Old Haven, to build it. The tower was occupied by Sergeant Miles Sweeney after the Napoleonic Wars, but was soon sold, together with the other Holland towers. They were auctioned at the Bell Inn in Thorpe, and demolished in 1820.

It is doubtful if the towers would have survived for long even if they had not been sold and demolished at this point. The coast at Holland was under severe threat, and 20 acres of land was said to have been lost here in the twenty years up to 1848. This indicates that the builders were severely lacking in local knowledge.

The bricks from the Holland towers were used to build five cottages and a bake house on land purchased from the lord of the manor by the parish.

Tower H

Also on Holland Marsh, Tower H did not have a supporting battery. It was occupied by Corporal William Stott after the Napoleonic Wars but was sold and demolished along with Tower G very soon afterwards. The tower stood on what is now a golf course.

An advertisement was placed in the *Ipswich Journal* in August 1819 for a large quantity of building material from the former Essex Martello towers, including oak joists and flooring, windows, doors and bricks. Mr Thompson of Great Holland was the contact.

Tower I

Tower I stood at Battery Point, Frinton. The area was named thus because a battery existed there before the tower. The land was bought from William Lushington of Tunbridge Wells, Kent. Occupied by William Dodds after the Napoleonic Wars, the tower was demolished in 1820.

An old view of the cliffs at Holland-on-Sea. The towers that once stood here were among the earliest to be destroyed.

Tower J

Tower J was built at Walton Cliffs, just above where the pier now stands. Walton-on-the-Naze was a very remote village at this time, so the building of a tower here was a major event. After the Napoleonic Wars ended the tower was occupied by Corporal Joseph Brown, and it was sold shortly after the previous three towers at Holland – for £1,255 in 1835. The safety of the tower had been in question from soon after its building, as the cliffs at this point had receded 40 yards between 1808 and 1826. The cliffs at Walton, especially round to the Naze, are still at risk, and the Naze tower (which pre-dates the Martello towers) is under threat, despite being some distance from the cliff edge. The sale of Tower J was advertised in the *Ipswich Journal* on 18 June 1834, and its site became a garden.

An interesting article in the *Colchester Gazette* of 30 November 2006 reported that builders working in Station Road, near Martello Road, had found tunnels that were once connected with the Martello tower. The report said that these had been dug to allow the garrison to escape if the tower was attacked or if there was an explosion there. This does not seem likely. Any tunnel entrance would have to have been in the basement, where the magazine was – and therefore the place most likely to be the scene of an explosion. The distance between Tower J and the next-nearest tower also makes the idea of them being connected unlikely.

Tower K

Tower K was built at Walton Backwaters overlooking Walton Creek, between Kirby Road and Mill Lane, on land bought from Peter Scaley. The Walton towers were in a remote position, as were the others in Essex. The fact that the tower was some distance from the main part of the town probably helped to ensure its survival, as the land was not needed for any other purpose and there seems to have been less danger from erosion here. In 1811 there were only forty-four houses and fifty-three families in the town.

After the Napoleonic Wars the tower had a distinguished occupant, a General Roff. *White's Gazetteer* of 1848 states that there was previously a tower on either side of the town but now there was only one, used by the Coastguard and as a signal station.

In 1859 Ford Madox Brown visited Walton and painted the tower from the high ground overlooking the Mere. His painting hangs in Birmingham Museum and Art Gallery. Although the tower was nearly forty years old, it was still occupied by the Army: two soldiers are pictured on the steps, a flag is flying and the gun is still in place. There were still fears of a French invasion at this time.

In common with many other towers, a modern gun was fitted during the First World War.

Tower K is now in the centre of a caravan site. Once used as a bar, it is now no longer in use, and is in poor condition.

Tower K, the only remaining tower in Walton-on-the-Naze. Now on the Martello caravan site.

Right: The doorway to Tower K, which was once used as a bar.

Below: An old photograph showing how the area around the Walton tower has developed over the years. This dates to before the First World War.

Harwich Redoubt

Harwich was a centre for naval shipbuilding, and its defences (including a wall around the town) dated back to the Middle Ages. From 1795 there were a semaphore station and barracks on Beacon Hill. More barracks were built in 1803 on Barrack Field. There was a plan to build a tower on Beacon Hill in 1798, but this did not materialise.

The presence of the Army in the town was not always an advantage. Violence often broke out between locals and the military, and sometimes among the soldiers themselves. When three companies of the 95th Rifles arrived in the town in 1808 they were only passing through on their way to Yarmouth, where they were to sail to Sweden to help stop the French invading that country. They were in Harwich long enough for two of the officers to fall out. Captain Brodie Grant and Lieutenant Jonathan Leyton settled their dispute by fighting a duel beneath the cliffs at Dovercourt, and Grant was shot and died. The Rifles then left to go abroad. When they returned Leyton was charged with murder, but he was acquitted.

The redoubt was built from 1808 to 1810, using French prisoners of war as a labour force, at a cost of £55,000. I have been unable to find out where the prisoners were housed for this period. One of the materials used was Roman cement, made from stone

Harwich Redoubt, which was derelict until taken over by the local volunteer group. The interior of the redoubt is similar to the one at Eastbourne.

quarried from the cliffs at Beacon Hill. This became a profitable business after the Napoleonic Wars, and went on until erosion of the cliffs (because of the works) caused silting of the harbour entrance.

The redoubt was sunk into a hill, so although it is on high ground it is partly protected by the raised banks around it. The road to Dovercourt had to be re-routed to make way for it. A large circular construction with walls 8 feet thick, there was a moat with a drawbridge, and the magazines were below ground level for added protection. It was armed with ten 24-pounder guns. Built as a command centre for Harwich, the redoubt could also be used to co-ordinate action at the local Martello towers – a similar role to that of the two South Coast redoubts.

The redoubt was still manned after the Napoleonic Wars ended: a receipt for 2 tons of straw delivered to the site by a Mr Clark survives. In 1848 there was a garrison of eighty men here, and in 1860 it was re-armed with 68-pounder guns. *White's Gazetteer* of 1848 goes into more detail. Not only were there eighty men and a captain, there were also a sergeant and two artillerymen. The redoubt is described by *White's* as the largest Martello tower in Britain. The *Gazetteer* also mentions a Royal Ordnance department near the High Lighthouse in Harwich, where the ammunition and guns for all the Essex towers were kept.

In October 1860 the first Essex Artillery Volunteers were inspected at the redoubt by Colonel Gibson of the Royal Artillery, having marched there led by a band. The colonel commented on the artillery experiments in Sussex that used Martello towers as targets, saying that he hoped they would be repeated in Essex, so the men could experience firing on the towers. Thankfully he never got his wish.

The late nineteenth century saw some improvements in the defences at Harwich, but these were mainly concentrated on Beacon Hill rather than the redoubt. However, two new guns were added in 1890 and some of the old guns were heaved over the defences into the moat, from where they were later dug out when the redoubt was modernised.

At one point in the First World War the redoubt was under the command of Lieutenant Ewing, who had returned wounded from France in 1918. Around 100 men were based here, and until disease put a stop to it they bred rabbits in the moat as an additional source of food. After the war the redoubt fell into disrepair, and the council built houses around it.

During the Second World War the redoubt was used for a time as a prison, and afterwards was taken over by the Civil Defence organisation, who carried out several nuclear exercises here. When they were disbanded it was left to decay. In the 1960s the council was prepared to sell the site to property developers, which aroused public interest in the building. The Harwich Society brought the redoubt back to a reasonable condition following its listing as an Ancient Monument. It is now open to the public as a museum, and includes a number of guns from different periods.

6

SUFFOLK

The coast of Suffolk, still quite remote in parts, was even more remote at the time of the Napoleonic Wars. This made it a prime site for French invasion, leading to the need for coastal defences. The threat to Suffolk (as with Essex) was primarily from a Dutch fleet carrying French troops from Holland, which in 1795 had become the French-controlled Batavian Republic.

In 1798 *A Military Memoir to Investigate the Defences of the Eastern District Including Suffolk* was written. It concluded that two sites in the county were seriously in danger of invasion – at Southwold, also known as Sole Bay, and Aldeburgh. Both these spots were favourable for landing troops, and were places where the Dutch had threatened the coast in previous conflicts. More surveys were to follow, and from higher authorities. *The Times* reported that in September 1801 the Duke of York left London to review the defences of the Essex, Suffolk and Norfolk coasts. As in other areas at risk of invasion, large numbers of troops were based here. In 1803 the 3rd Regiment of Foot was stationed at Bromeswell Heath, before moving to Hollesey and Orford. Aldeburgh became a large military camp in case of Napoleon's arrival, and naval vessels were based off the Suffolk coast.

On 11 July 1803 a meeting attended by the Lord Lieutenant of Suffolk, Lord Euston, was held at the White Hart Inn at Stowmarket. In the event of invasion, the plan was to divide the county into two or three districts, each under the control of a deputy lieutenant, hopefully a magistrate. If an invasion took place they were in charge of implementing the agreed actions. Plans were also made for a system of communications to be set up in the county.

If the *Ipswich Journal* is to be believed, the level of patriotism rose in relation to the danger of invasion. The newspaper published a song that was apparently being sung by soldiers in their tents as they waited for the invasion to begin. The first verse:

Eve of Invasion
The hour of battle now draws nigh
We swear to conquer or to die
Haste quick away thou slow paced night
Tomorrow's dawn begins the fight

In their 1805 report the Royal Engineers recommended that a number of towers be built along the coast at various points: thirty-two in Essex and twenty-six in Suffolk, including eight between the Debden River and Orford Haven. As with Essex, the Sussex towers were numbered – not given an identifying letter.

In May 1806 an inspection of the area by a Major Bryce was ordered by General Morse, the Inspector General of Fortifications. Bryce recognised that the Suffolk coast needed fortifications but thought that these should be forts. General Morse decided that Martello towers should be built instead. As in other areas, towers were seen by most people at this time as the best option, because of their cost and because of their staying power in the face of an attack. Morse suggested that there should be two large eight-gun towers at Orford and Slaughden, similar to the redoubts built in the other three counties that were to have towers or already had them. These large towers were never built.

The *Ipswich Journal* of July 1808 reported that a considerable quantity of building materials for the Martello towers to be built on Suffolk's coast had already been landed. The towers that were built (apart from the last one) were all three-gun types, similar to the Essex towers. They either had three 24-pounders or one 24-pounder and two 5½-inch howitzers. A number also had supporting batteries, with large numbers of troops based in barracks at places such as Woodbridge. Much troop movement was necessary to man the towers. In June 1811, 200 members of the Hertford Militia went to Shotley, while Felixstowe saw the arrival of 500 members of the Cumberland Militia, and the Dumfries Militia marched from Woodbridge Barracks to Aldeburgh. They obviously didn't stay long, as in October the West Norfolk Militia marched from Aldeburgh to Woodbridge Barracks.

The Suffolk towers were in communication with each other and with positions further inland, while tar barrels were kept ready to be used as beacons if the invasion came. There was also a telegraph system at the Bawdsey Ferry tower which could communicate with Woodbridge. Locals panicked when this system was tested, thinking that the invasion had happened.

Although the bricks for the Suffolk towers mainly came from London, some were made locally in the brickyards at Snape and Aldeburgh. It is likely that some of the bricks from London were carried by local craft, such as the *Industrious Ann* and the *Farmer's Delight*, spritsail barges owned by local farmers.

A number of the towers were re-armed in 1862 with 68-pounders.

Tower L

Tower L and Tower M were built on Bloody Point at Shotley. Tower L, which supported an existing battery, overlooked the River Stour at Shotley Gate and controlled the entry of ships into the river. It was later incorporated into HMS *Ganges*, the naval training ship (which had barracks on land as well), and was used as a signal base by the establishment.

In 1861 a detachment of two sergeants and twenty-eight other ranks of the Royal Artillery, led by Lieutenant T. B. Berthon, arrived from Woolwich to mount 68-pounder guns on the towers.

Tower L, the first Suffolk tower at Shotley, overlooking the River Stour on the old HMS *Ganges* site.

The naval school closed in the 1970s and was sold to private owners. Tower L has survived, although *Ganges* has not. Part of it was converted into a police training centre, which was used by a number of police forces, but this closed in the early 1990s and the area was sold again. There seems to be some dispute over what is going to happen to the site, and at present the whole of what was HMS *Ganges* is fenced off and derelict. A few buildings outside the fence have been converted into flats. The tower can be seen from the road nearby. A strange green construction with a pointed roof has been added to the top.

Tower M

Tower M stood on the other side of Shotley Point, overlooking the River Orwell, and controlled ships entering the river, which runs up to Ipswich. It was let to private tenants after the Napoleonic Wars, but eventually became part of HMS *Ganges* and was used as a water tower; the water tank is still on top of it and vertical cracks in the walls indicate that this extra weight has caused some damage to the structure.

In 1898 the towers at Shotley were manned by infantry and artillery to guard against hostile forces entering the harbour. Like Tower L, Tower M is situated inside the derelict HMS *Ganges*, overlooking what is now Shotley Marina.

Tower M, on the opposite side of the *Ganges* site to Tower L, overlooking the River Orwell.

Tower N

Tower N was opposite Tower M, on the other side of the Orwell at Walton Ferry. This was one of the towers that had a moat. It supported a battery in 1872, and was still an important part of the Harwich defences.

After the Second World War the tower was derelict, and the huge container port built on this site has removed any visual record of it.

Tower O

Tower O was at Langer Point near Landguard Fort, which seems a strange place for a tower when a fort had been established here for hundreds of years. It was used as a powder magazine in 1818, but was a victim of erosion in the 1870s.

Tower P

West of Felixstowe seafront, Tower P was given to the Coastguard in 1816. In April 1907 an agreement was made between the Admiralty and the Felixstowe and Walton Urban District Council which allowed the council to erect meteorological instruments here, when it was still a Coastguard station. Four thermometers were placed on a stand, and instruments on a brick pier on the roof of the tower recorded sunshine levels. The cost of the agreement was 2s 6d per annum, to be paid every January without

Tower P in Felixstowe situated on what is known as Wireless Green.

any deductions, and the first payment to be made in advance. Council staff were not allowed to enter the tower without written permission, data being recorded by the Coastguard men stationed there.

The tower was used as a wireless station for ships based at Harwich during the First World War, and the area where it stands became known as Wireless Green. The destroyers of the Harwich fleet played a major role in the war in the North Sea, and after the war ended the harbour was full of surrendered German U-Boats.

The tower has been neglected for some years and in 2006 there was a meeting involving the local council and English Heritage to discuss plans for it. Similar discussions had taken place over the previous twenty years, and a condition survey had been carried out in 2003, concluding that the tower was South Felixstowe's only significant historical asset. One idea that came out of the meeting was that the tower should be turned into an arts centre, no doubt similar to the one at Jaywick in Essex (Tower D). This was not popular with all local residents, some of whom thought that any work carried out should reflect the historical aspect of the tower.

The *Ipswich Evening Star* in March 2007 reported that the tower was to become a 'Window on the World', an arts, education and discovery centre that would allow contact with communities around the world – but this idea is now on hold.

Currently there are plans to build a large number of houses around the tower, proposed by the council in partnership with private enterprise. The tower would be in the centre of a park, and repairs would be paid for by the private builder. However, these plans are subject to constant change. The *Evening Star* of 1 April 2009 stated that the houses would have to be half a metre higher than originally planned, with an extra three steps up to them, to avoid flooding – caused by rising sea levels. In an extreme flood event, though, the ground floors may still be flooded. The *Star* article does not mention what effects this may have on the tower itself.

Tower Q

Tower Q was built near Bull's Cliff to support an existing battery, and until just before the First World War it was used as a position-finding marker by Landguard Fort. In 1842 Felixstowe church bazaar was held at the tower, which was lent by the proprietors Robert Garrod and George Mason.

An advertisement in the *Ipswich Journal* stated that Felixstowe estate in east Suffolk was for sale. It had a frontage to the German Ocean (as the North Sea used to be called) and two Martello towers north of Landguard Fort.

The tower was later used as an exhibition room and tea room. There are a number of posters now in the Suffolk Record Office that advertise this. One mentions an exhibition about how the towers were built, and advertises cream teas. Another mentions that the tearoom and garden were situated in the tower's dry moat. Until the tower was converted into a residence in 1946 it still had a moat and a drawbridge.

In April 2008 a 250-year-old cannon was found in the moat of Tower Q, and a crane had to be brought in to lift it out. This may have been from the tower or from a nearby

Tower Q is a very elegant home, difficult to find among the modern homes around it.

battery, but it is unlikely to have been from the tower unless old guns were used to arm them.

The tower is situated in a built-up area, and it is quite difficult to find as it is surrounded by houses. Part of the moat wall is still in place, but with a gap for the driveway from the road. A cannon stands at the end of the drive – perhaps the one from the moat.

Tower R

Tower R stood on the cliffs at Felixstowe and like Tower Q was used as a position-finding marker for Landguard Fort. It was supposedly demolished in the early twentieth century. It has, however, since been discovered that half of the tower still exists as part of the Bartlett Hospital.

Tower S

Tower S was on the cliffs about half a mile from Tower R. It was abandoned in 1835, shortly after it was built, because coastal erosion was making it dangerous. A report in the *Ipswich Journal* in August 1844 said that the taking of cement stone from the foot of cliffs 2½ miles north-east of the town had led to the erosion of a ledge that had formed a breakwater. Two Martello towers and a battery have now gone into the sea.

Tower R was thought to have been destroyed but half of the tower is now part of the Bartlett Hospital. (Steve Popple)

Tower T

Built at the River Debden near Woodbridge Haven, Tower T supported a battery. It is clearly visible from the site of Bawdsey Manor on the opposite side of the river. The tower was used by the Coastguard in the early twentieth century and is now on the golf course at Felixstowe Ferry. It is currently unused.

Tower U

Also built on the Debden, Tower U is further into the river mouth. There was a long-running court case over this tower in the late 1870s. A Colonel Tomline believed that he owned the land around the tower, and had begun to take shingle from the beach. The government contested this, saying that they owned the tower and that removing shingle could lead to erosion of the tower. The government must have won as the tower is still there. It stands opposite Bawdsey Manor, where radar was developed during the Second World War, and is now a residence.

Tower V

Tower V was built on the other side of the River Debden, facing Tower U. It stood in the grounds of Bawdsey Manor and was sold to Lord Dysart in 1820, as he owned the

Tower T stands at Woodbridge Haven on the River Debden. It is now on the golf course at Felixstowe Ferry. (Steve Popple)

Tower U is further into the mouth of the River Debden than the previous tower. It has now been turned into a residence. (Steve Popple)

land it stood on. The land that Tower U and Tower V were built on was rented from him for 5s a year.

The tower was demolished shortly after the end of the Napoleonic Wars. Near its site is a more modern form of defence, the nuclear bunker at Bawdsey.

Tower W

This stands on the cliffs at Bawdsey and was let to private tenants after the end of the Napoleonic Wars. In recent years it has been in great danger because of cliff erosion. In 2005, 46 feet of the cliff edge disappeared in eight months. The owners of the tower were very worried about this, but an article at the time reported that the Environment Agency was to spend £1.5 million on coastal protection for this area – which will help to protect the nearby Second World War defences as well as the Martello tower.

When I visited in November 2009 it was not possible to get very close as the pathway has collapsed. It would seem that the tower is still in great danger.

Tower X

Tower X was built on the lower ground in the south of Bawdsey. The tower was let to private tenants after the war. It vanished in the nineteenth century but its base was used to house a gun during the Second World War. There are several Second World War

Tower W is on the cliffs at Bawdsey. It is in a very dangerous position due to cliff erosion. When I visited in 2009 part of the path leading to it was closed because it had collapsed. (Steve Popple)

The coastline from close to Tower W. Towers Y, Z and AA are visible.

Some of the Second World War defences built between Towers W and Y. The remains of Tower X lie beneath one of the more modern defences.

defensive structures along this section of coast, but it is hard to judge which one is on the Martello site.

Standing near the location of this tower it is possible to see Tower W to the south and three towers to the north, Tower Y, Tower Z and Tower AA, although the last (at Shingle Street) is quite some distance away. This gives some idea of how parts of the East and South Coast must have looked when the towers were built, uninterrupted by new buildings.

Tower Y

This was another tower built at Bawdsey, and let to private tenants after the war. This is another tower for which little history is recorded. It is now unoccupied. There is some kind of structure on the top, which looks like part of the living quarters. It is quite surprising that this tower is still used, as it is in a very remote position.

Tower Z

At Alderton, Tower Z was let to private tenants after the war. Little seems to be known about the tower. It is now empty and remote but seems to be in good conditions although English Heritage consider it to be in danger. The village sign for Alderton has the Martello on it in a prominent position.

Above left: Tower Y has been converted into accommodation but is in a very remote position. (Steve Popple)

Above right: Tower Z is at Alderton. The village sign has a Martello tower on it. Now deserted, the tower seems to be in decline. (Steve Popple)

Towers Y and Z. Tower ZZ at Shingle Street lies off to the far right.

Tower AA

Tower AA stands at Shingle Street. It is probably one of the most remote of all the towers. There seem to have been no residents here at all until the tower was built, at which point several fishermen (who also worked as pilots) built huts from driftwood.

The tower was occupied by the Coastguard after the Napoleonic Wars, but later cottages were built for the Coastguard men. The 1841 census for the area shows that only pilots and coastguards lived here, including nine people in the tower: the Harris and McDermott families, who were of Irish origin. Many members of the Coastal Blockade on the South Coast were recruited from Ireland, and it looks as if the Coastguard might have had a large Irish contingent as well. By the 1851 census there was only one family in the tower. John Bunguard from Sussex was head of the family. He was a coastguard, and some of his children had other occupations. The 1861 census tells us that the tower was occupied by James Friend, a sergeant tower keeper, Chelsea pensioner and coastguard. Other coastguards lived at Shingle Street, at Battery House, Watch Tower and in nearby cottages.

As late as 1888 this remote position was still a cause for concern: even then it was an ideal spot for the landing of an enemy force. A telegraph station was planned to connect the area with Woodbridge Barracks.

Shingle Street is rumoured to have been the site of an invasion not during the Napoleonic Wars but in the Second World War. By that time the area had been emptied of civilian residents, and only the Army knew what really happened – and papers relating to the event have not yet been released by the government.

The tower has been converted and is now a home. The area is still very remote and the few houses that stand there are mainly holiday homes.

Tower AA at Shingle Street. It is now a residence in the remote village. The few houses here are the only habitation for some distance, showing the need for towers on this remote coast.

Tower BB

Tower BB was built close to the River Ore, but was demolished in 1822, shortly after the Napoleonic Wars, because of erosion.

Tower CC

There is a huge gap between Tower BB and Tower CC, the final tower in Suffolk: they are almost 10 miles apart. This is similar to the final tower at the other end of the line at Seaford, which also stands on its own.

Tower CC is at Slaghden near Aldeburgh on the estuary of the River Alde. Not only is it remote, but it is also different from every other tower as it is shaped like a cloverleaf. Originally planned as an eight-gun tower, it finally only had four.

The tower was turned into a house in the 1930s, when an elegant superstructure was added, but was requisitioned during the Second World War and used as an observation post. It was bought by the Landmark Trust in 1971 and restored (the 1930s addition was removed), and is now available to rent as a holiday home – although it is very close to the sea and is under threat from coastal erosion. The wall around the moat is still in place, apart from on the side facing the sea. There is a much later sea wall along the beach, and it would seem either that part of the original wall was removed to allow the building of this or had already been lost through erosion.

Tower CC is the last tower, but there were nearly more further north. There are plans in the National Archives for a proposed tower at the entrance to Great Yarmouth harbour, which was to be built in 1839.

Tower CC is the most unusual tower of all the towers on the East and South Coasts due to its structure.

Appendix 1

Surviving Towers

Kent

Tower 1	Home
Tower 2	Home
Tower 3	Museum
Tower 4	Unused
Tower 5	Unused
Tower 6	Unused
Tower 7	Unused
Tower 8	Home
Tower 9	Unused
Tower 13	Home
Tower 14	Unused
Tower 19	Unused
Tower 23	Home
Tower 24	Museum
Tower 25	Unused

Sussex

Tower 28	Unused
Tower 30	Unused
Tower 55	Unused
Tower 60	Home
Tower 61	Unused
Tower 62	Home
Tower 64	Unused
Tower 66	Unused
Tower 73	Museum
Tower 74	Museum

Essex

Tower A	Museum
Tower C	Resource Centre
Tower D	Unused
Tower E	Unused
Tower F	Restaurant (currently closed)
Tower K	Unused

Suffolk

Tower L	Unused
Tower M	Unused
Tower P	Unused
Tower Q	Home
Tower T	Unused
Tower U	Home
Tower W	Unused
Tower Y	Unused
Tower Z	Unused
Tower AA	Home
Tower CC	Home

APPENDIX 2

LOST TOWERS

Although I have tried to find the exact dates that the towers disappeared, this has not always been possible. Therefore I have grouped together the towers that are recorded as disappearing in the middle of the nineteenth century, those that disappeared in the late nineteenth century and those that disappeared in the early twentieth century.

V	Demolished because of danger from erosion in 1819
29	Victim of erosion just after construction around 1820
G	Demolished because of danger from erosion in 1820
H	Demolished because of danger from erosion in 1820
I	Demolished because of danger from erosion in 1820
BB	Fell to erosion in 1822
J	Demolished because of danger from erosion in 1836
45	Victim of erosion in 1839
27	Demolished in 1841
41	Demolished in 1842
S	Erosion in the mid-nineteenth century
31	Erosion in the mid-nineteenth century
32	Erosion in the mid-nineteenth century
34	Erosion in the mid-nineteenth century
47	Erosion in the mid-nineteenth century
72	Probably a victim of erosion in the mid-nineteenth century
48	Demolished in 1858
71	Destroyed by weapon testing in 1860
50	Destroyed by weapon testing in 1860
49	Possibly destroyed by same tests as Tower 50 in 1860
37	Demolished in 1864
42	Demolished in 1868
10	Demolished in 1869 for the construction of the promenade at Hythe
11	Demolished in 1869 for the construction of the promenade at Hythe
12	Demolished in 1869 for the construction of the promenade at Hythe
46	Demolished in 1870
O	Erosion in the 1870s
26	Demolished in 1871

35	Demolished in 1872
36	Demolished in 1872
38	Demolished in 1872
40	Demolished in 1873
70	Destroyed by artillery testing in 1876
39	Demolished in 1876
33	Blown up in 1889
X	Erosionin the late nineteenth century
51	Erosion in the late nineteenth century
52	Erosion in the late nineteenth century
53	Erosion in the late nineteenth century
56	Erosion in the late nineteenth century
69	Erosion in the late nineteenth century
59	Demolished in 1903
54	Demolished in 1908
68	Demolished in 1910
58	Demolished in the early twentieth century
R	Partly demolished in the early twentieth century
57	Erosion in the early twentieth century
16	Erosion in the early twentieth century
17	Erosion in the early twentieth century
18	Erosion in the early twentieth century
20	Erosion in the early twentieth century
21	Erosion in the early twentieth century
43	Erosion in the early twentieth century
44	Erosion in the early twentieth century
67	Demolished in the 1920s
65	Erosion in the 1930s
63	Demolished during the Second World War
N	Demolished after the Second World War
22	Demolished in 1956
B	Demolished in 1967

Appendix 3

Signal Towers

A series of coastal signal towers were built in 1795. They made it possible for information to be sent over long distances very quickly. Each tower was commanded by a naval lieutenant on half pay, who was also paid 7s 6d a day. There were also a midshipman (at 2s a day and the rate for a fourth-rate vessel) and two seamen (at 2s a day).

This appendix lists the towers and the tower lieutenants who were in command. Where possible I have added the county but could not find the position of all of the towers.

Ashey Down	Isle of Wight, Charles Morgan
Ballard Hill	Dorset, William Osborne
Berry Head	Devon, D. P. Cumby
Blackhead	Arthur Hayne
Christchurch Yard	Dorset, Richard Jewers
Dodman	Cornwall, Richard Collier
Dunnose	Isle of Wight, Samuel Codd
Gurnose	Nicholas Hoare
Hambro Hill	Essex, John Watts
Hurters Top	R. Mitchell
Land's End	Cornwall, John May
Lizard	Cornwall, Samuel Barnsley
Maker	George Hire
Manacle Point	Cornwall, John Dixon
Nealand	John Mackenzie
Needle Point	Isle of Wight, Philip Justice
Park Lough	William Alsray
Portland	Dorset, Arthur Clark
Punch Knoll	Henry Rostler
Round Down	Christopher Roberts
Start Point	William Clements
St Alban's Head	Dorset, William Pasty
St Anthony's Head	Cornwall, Walter Jewell
St Catherine's	Jersey, Robert Wilson

St Leven's Point	Charles Le Caree
Totterdug Mount	A. Loisey
West Down Beacon	Devon, George Dundas
West Sore	H. Y. Darracott
Whitelands	William Read
Thackhead	Arthur Hayne

BIBLIOGRAPHY

Arnott, W. G., *Alde Estuary* (Boydell Press, 1973)

Bloomfield, Peter, *Kent and the Napoleonic Wars* (Alan Sutton Publishing, 1987)

Boreham, B., 'Martello Towers' (Folkestone Local History Leaflet No. 1)

Boyden, P., *Walton 1800–1867* (Walton Records Office, 1981)

Centre For Kentish Studies, P125/7/2 Dymchurch Parish Records

Clements, W. H., *Towers of Strength* (Leo Cooper, 1999)

Cobbett, William, *Rural Rides* (Penguin, 2001)

Cochrane, Lord Admiral, *The Memoirs of a Fighting Captain* (Folio Society, 2005)

De Sélincourt, Aubrey, *The Channel Shore* (Robert Hale, 1953)

Douch, John, *Smuggling: Flogging Joey's Warriors* (Crabwell & Buckland Publications, 1985)

East Sussex Record Office, CUS 1/1/8 'Towers Occupied by the Coast Guard' (1852)

East Sussex Record Office, CUS 1/1/7 'Coast Blockade Report'

East Sussex Record Office, PEV/99 'Order For Quarter Sessions'

Elleray, D. Robert, *Eastbourne* (Phillimore, 1995)

Enoch, Victor J., *The Martello Towers of Ireland* (Eason & Sons Ltd, 1975)

Essex Record Office, D/DR P18 Map of Great Clacton

Essex Record Office, D/DR T108 Deeds of Jaywick Farm

Essex Record Office, D/B 6 M21/1 Minutes of Borough & Port Health Committee

Essex Record Office, T/A 218/1 'Military Memoir on the Defence of the Eastern District' (1798)

Essex Record Office, T/A 218/1 'A Report on the Defences of the County of Essex Against Invasion' (1804)

Essex Record Office, T/2/ 561/42/1 'Essex During The French Wars'

Fereday, R. P., *The Longhope Battery and Towers* (R. P. Fereday, 1971)

George, Michael and Martin, *Coast of Conflict* (SB Publications, 2004)

Glascock, Captain W. N., *Naval Sketch Book, Service Afloat and Ashore* (Colburn & Bentley, 1831)

Glendinning, I., *The Hammers of Invicta* (Glendinning, 1981)

Glyn-Forest, D., *Martello Tower* (Frederick Warne, 1946)

Grimsley, E. J., *The Historical Development of the Martello Tower in the Channel Islands* (Go Guernsey Publication, 1988)

Hastings News, 9 October 1868, 3 June 1870, 26 April 1872, 14 July 1876,
    5 December 1873

Hogg, I., *The History of Fortification* (Orbis, 1981)

Hutchinson, Geoff, *Martello Towers* (G. Hutchinson, 1994)

Ipswich Journal, 16 June 1808, 23 July 1808, 14 August 1819, 20 April 1844,
    25 August 1860, 27 July 1861, 18 January 1868

Jacobs, N., *The Sunshine Coast* (Tyndale & Panda, 1986)

Kent, Peter, *Fortifications of East Anglia* (Terence Dalton, 1988)

Kitchen, F., 'The Guns of Hythe', *Bygone Kent* Vol. 10, No. 4 (1989)

Lewis-Stempel, John, *The Autobiography of the British Soldier* (Headline Review,
    2007)

Lloyd, Peter A., *The French Are Coming! The Invasion Scare 1803–05* (Spellmount,
    1991)

Manchester Guardian, 18 December 1859, 28 December 1867, 28 July 1926

Maurice-Jones, Colonel K. W., *The History of Coast Artillery in the British Army* (The
    Naval & Military Press)

Mead, Commander P., 'The Martello Towers of England', article from unknown book

Milton, R. and R. Callaghan, *The Redoubt Fortress and Martello Towers of
    Eastbourne* (Eastbourne Local History Society, 2005)

Morning Chronicle, 15 November 1821

National Archives, WO 33/25 'Report of Committee on Coastal Defences' (1873)

National Archives, WO 33/9 'Breaching Experiment With Armstrong Gun Against a
    Martello Tower at Eastbourne'

National Archives, WO 80/8 Sir George Murray Papers

National Archives, MPH 1/1175/8 Plan of Rye Harbour

National Archives, NA MPHH 1/593 'The Defences on the Sussex Coast near
    Eastbourne'

National Archives, MR 1/1409 'Topographical Survey of Sussex'

National Archives, ADM 49/21 Coastal Blockade Papers

National Archives, ADM 106/3506 Navy Board Records

Observer, 4 March 1822

Philip, R., *The Coast Blockade* (Compton Press, 1999)

Rose, C. and J. Astell, *The Martello Tower at Seaford* (Newhaven & Seaford
    Historical Society, 1970)

Saunders, Andrew, *Channel Defences* (Batsford, 1997)

Shenstone, J. C., 'A Yeoman's Common-Place Book at the Commencement of the
    Nineteenth Century', *Essex Review*, Vol. xxii

Spears, H. D., *Local Martello Towers* (Spears, 1974)

Suffolk Record Office, HD 2272191/10/4 'Wars and warfare – Martello Tower'

Suffolk Record Office, HD 2272191/10/3 'Wars and warfare – Martello Tower'

Suffolk Record Office, HD 672/1/124 'Notes and news cuttings Martello Towers'

Suffolk Record Office, EF 12/1/7/1/2 Memorandum of Agreement

Sutcliffe, Sheila, *Martello Towers* (David and Charles, 1972)

Sussex Chronicle, 22 October 1821, 24 November 1860

Telling, R. M., *English Martello Towers* (CST Books, 1997)

Telling, R. M., *Handbook on Martello Towers* (CST Books, 1998)

The Times, 9 September 1795, 3 October 1804, 23 March 1805, 24 October 1806, 26 February 1822, 7 January 1828, 29 August 1829, 27 August 1857, 9 August 1860, 29 October 1860, 7 November 1876, 22 September 1919, 21 June 1932, 6 September 1934

Thomas, Dorothy K. and Ruth I. Johns, *Dorothy from Hythe in Kent* (Plowright Press, 2004)

Walker, Kenneth, 'Martello Towers and the Defence of North East Essex in the Napoleonic War', *Essex Review* (October 1938)

Walker, Kenneth, *The History of the Martello Tower* (Clacton On Sea: Clacton Urban District Council)

Waugh, Mary, *Smuggling in Kent and Sussex 1700–1840* (Countryside Books, 1985)

Weekly Political Register, 13 September 1823

Yarrow, A., *The Fortifications of East Sussex* (East Sussex County Planning Department, 1979)

ALSO AVAILABLE FROM AMBERLEY PUBLISHING

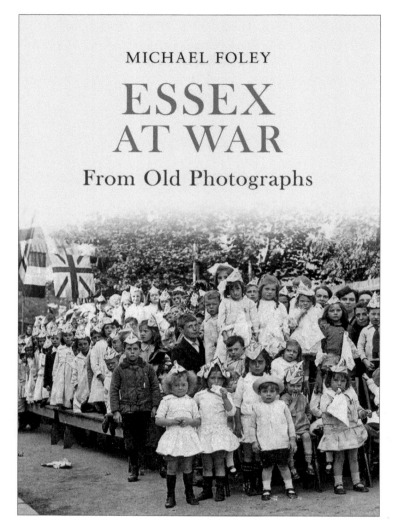

Essex at War From Old Photographs
Michael Foley

From the remains of ancient castles through to the Napoleonic
Martello towers, the perilous history of Essex can be seen in all
corners of the county. Many of the military structures of Essex are
illustrated in this fascinating collection of photographs.

978 1 84868 618 2
128 pages, 100 b&w images

Available from all good bookshops or order direct
from our website www.amberleybooks.com